PAINT SHOP PRO

in easy steps

Stephen Copestake

COMPUTER STEP

In easy steps is an imprint of Computer Step
Southfield Road. Southam
Warwickshire CV47 OFB. England

Tel: 01926 817999 Fax: 01926 817005
http://www.computerstep.com

Second edition 2000
First edition 1998

Notice of Liability
Every effort has been made to ensure that this book contains accurate
and current information. However, Computer Step and the author shall
not be liable for any loss or damage suffered by readers as a result of
any information contained herein.

Trademarks
Paint Shop Pro™ is a trademark of Jasc Software Incorporated. All
other trademarks are acknowledged as belonging to their respective
companies.

Printed and bound in the United Kingdom

ISBN 1-84078-054-1

Contents

4 **Using filters** **87**

5   Using deformations   125

6   Using effects   145

7 Advanced techniques   165

Index   187

First steps

In this chapter, you'll learn how to use the Paint Shop Pro screen; open existing files; create new ones; save changes to disk; and export images for use on the Web. You'll rescale images, and resize the underlying canvas, then go on to learn about image formats and special screen modes. You'll also zoom in and out on images, and reverse/redo image amendments. Finally, you'll learn how to work with background/foreground colours.

Covers

Chapter One

The Paint Shop Pro screen

You can have Paint Shop Pro apply a grid to images. Grids are a structure of horizontal/vertical lines which you can use to align objects more accurately:

Part of a grid

To view (or hide) the grid, press Ctrl+Alt+G.

The Paint Shop Pro screen is exceptionally easy to use. When you run the program, this is the result:

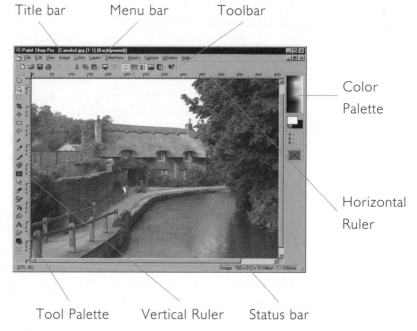

Title bar Menu bar Toolbar

Color Palette

Horizontal Ruler

Tool Palette Vertical Ruler Status bar

The following are details of screen components specific to Paint Shop Pro:

The other components are common to most or all Windows programs. See your Windows documentation for how to use them.

The Toolbar

This is a collection of icons. By clicking an appropriate icon, you can launch a specific feature.

Many other screen features (e.g. the Status bar and Color Palette) are also classed as toolbars.

The Tool Palette

A specialised toolbar which you use to launch a variety of tools (e.g. the Zoom tool – see page 20).

The Color Palette

An easy and convenient way to access Paint Shop Pro's colour selection tools (see pages 24-25).

Customising screen components

To view or hide a toolbar, follow step 1 but select Toolbars instead. Do the following:

B Click here

A Select or deselect one or more toolbars

(You can also use this method to hide the Tool and Color Palettes.)

Step 1 also hides the Grid or Rulers, as appropriate.

To hide the Status bar, right-click the Tool Palette and select Status Bar.

You can use two techniques to specify which screen components display:

The menu route

Pull down the View menu and do the following:

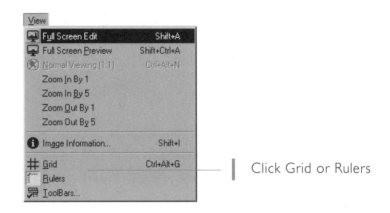

Click Grid or Rulers

The Toolbar route

In the on-screen Toolbar, do the following as appropriate:

Click here to show/
hide the Tool Palette

Click here to show/
hide the Color Palette

Opening files

If you open a vector format, a second dialog may open after step 2 e.g.:

Complete the dialog, then click OK.

Paint Shop Pro will open (i.e. read and display) over 40 separate graphics file formats. These fall into two broad categories: raster and vector – see page 19 for details of some of the principal image formats supported by Paint Shop Pro. When you tell Paint Shop Pro to open an image, it automatically recognises which format it was written to, and acts accordingly. It does this by taking account of the file suffix. For example, for TIFF (Tagged Image File Format) images to be opened in Paint Shop Pro, they must end in:

.TIF

Not all of the supported formats, however, can be written to disk. (See pages 16-17 for how to save/export files.)

You open files via the Open dialog, or via a special Browser.

To preview your image before you open it, ensure Show Preview is activated (as here).

Opening images – the dialog route

| Pull down the File menu and click Open

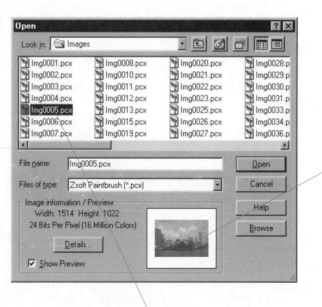

Image Preview

Before you carry out step 2, do the following:

- **use the Look in: field to locate the drive which hosts the file you want to open, and;**
- **(if necessary) double-click one or more folders until you locate the relevant file**

2 Double-click a graphics file

...cont'd

 You can also use the Browser for file housekeeping.
   Press Ctrl+B if the Browser isn't on-screen. Then simply right-click any image thumbnail on the right of the Browser and do any of the following:

- **to rename the image, click Rename. In the Rename File dialog, type in the new name and click OK**
- **to copy the image, click Copy To. In the Browse for Folder dialog, type in the destination folder and click OK, or;**
- **to delete the image, click Delete. In the message which appears, click Yes to confirm the deletion**

   To close the Browser, press Ctrl+F4.

Opening images – the Browser route

1 Follow step 1 on the facing page

2 Carry out the procedures in the DON'T FORGET tip on the facing page

3 Click this button: Browse

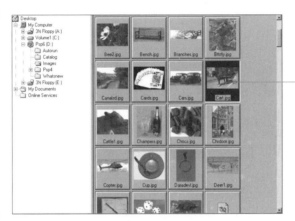

4 Double-click an image

The opened image:

Resizing files

Pixels (a contraction of 'picture element') **are dots, the smallest element which can be displayed on screen. Bitmapped graphics consist of pixels; each is allocated a colour (or greyscale).**

Paint Shop Pro lets you resize an image. You can do this in three ways:

- by altering the pixel dimensions

- by restating the dimensions as a percentage of the original

- by changing the image resolution (called 'resampling')

Resizing an image

1 Pull down the Image menu and click Resize

2 Perform step 3, 4 OR 5. Finally, carry out step 6:

Re step 5 – increasing the resolution **reduces the image size (and vice versa).**

3 Click here, then amend the associated Width or Height fields

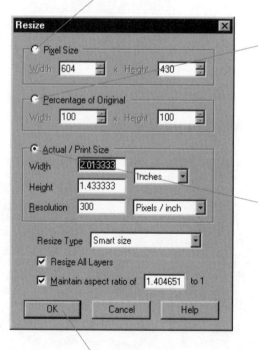

Resize	
◯ Pixel Size	
Width 604 x Height 430	
◯ Percentage of Original	
Width 100 x Height 100	
◉ Actual / Print Size	
Width 2.013333	Inches
Height 1.433333	
Resolution 300	Pixels / inch
Resize Type Smart size	
☑ Resize All Layers	
☑ Maintain aspect ratio of 1.404651 to 1	
OK Cancel Help	

To select a new resizing type, click **the Resize Type field. In the list, select a type.**

4 Click here, then amend the associated Width or Height fields

5 Click here, then type in a new resolution in the Resolution field

Resizing bitmaps produces some level **of distortion. The trick is to minimise this as far as possible.**

6 Click here

New files

To duplicate the active image, click its Title bar. Press Shift+D; Paint Shop Pro opens the copy in its own (new) window.

Often, images will be 'ready-made' for you, in the sense that you'll:

- open existing images (see pages 10-11)

- create screenshots by carrying out screen captures (see Chapter 7)

- duplicate existing images (see the HOT TIP)

However, there will be times when you'll need to create an image from scratch. There are several stages, but Paint Shop Pro makes this easy:

Resolution is defined as the measurement (usually expressed in linear dpi – dots per inch) of image sharpness.

1. launching the New Image dialog

2. specifying the width and height, in pixels

3. selecting a background colour

4. specifying the resolution

5. selecting an image type (including the number of colours)

Creating a new image

Pull down the File menu and do the following:

Click here

Now carry out the following steps:

To specify the image resolution, type it in here:

Re the above tip – use the following suggestions as guidelines:

- **Web pictures – use a resolution of 72 pixels per inch, and;**
- **other pictures – use the range 96-150 pixels per inch (this is a useful standard)**

2 Complete the Width and Height fields

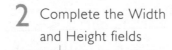

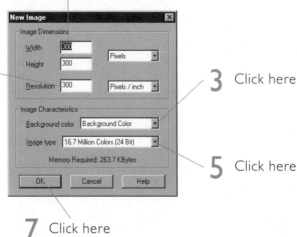

3 Click here

5 Click here

7 Click here

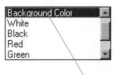

4 Select a background colour

6 Select an image type

The resulting image:

A new, blank image (the background colour is white) in its own window

Enlarging an image's canvas

 Note that enlarging an image's canvas (unlike resizing) does not expand the image itself.

As we've seen on pages 13-14, when you can create an image from scratch, you specify the width and height in pixels. When you do this, Paint Shop Pro automatically defines a 'canvas' (the area on which the image lies) with the same dimensions. However, you can easily specify increased dimensions for the canvas.

Increasing an image's canvas

1 Pull down the Image menu and click Canvas Size

 Before you carry out steps 1-3 here, first follow steps 2-4 on page 25 to select a background colour.

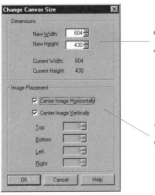

2 Complete the New Width and/or New Height fields

3 Optional – select either or both of these to centre the image within the new canvas

 Re step 3 – if you don't select both centring options, also complete the relevant placement boxes:

Top: -106

Bottom: -106

Left: -146

Right: -147

Canvas enlargement in action:

Here, the canvas has been enlarged vertically and horizontally

In this instance, the background is white

Saving files

Re step 1 – Paint Shop Pro has its own proprietary format (suffix: .PSP) which retains:

- **layers**
- **vectors**
- **masks, and;**
- **selection data**

Use the PSP format while you're working with an image; when it's complete, save it to the nonproprietary format of your choice.

Re. step 1 – many image formats have sub-formats and/or compression options you can choose from.

If it's available, click this button immediately after step 1:

Options...

In the resulting dialog, select the appropriate option(s). Click OK.

When you're working on one or more images in Paint Shop Pro, it's important to save your work at frequent intervals, in order to avoid data loss in the event of a hardware fault or power interruption.

Saving a file for the first time

Pull down the File menu and click Save. Now do the following:

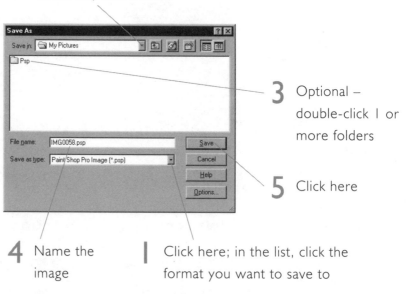

2 Click here; in the drop-down list, click a drive

3 Optional – double-click 1 or more folders

5 Click here

4 Name the image

1 Click here; in the list, click the format you want to save to

Saving previously saved files

Pull down the File menu and click Save. No dialog launches; instead, Paint Shop Pro saves the latest version of your file to disk, overwriting the previous.

Saving copies of images

You can also save a copy of the active picture (and leave the original intact).

Pull down the File menu and click Save Copy As. Now follow steps 1-5 above.

Exporting files for the Internet

 Formats suitable for Web use include:

- **GIF**
- **JPEG, and;**
- **PNG**

See page 19 for more information.

You can use steps 1-5 on the facing page to produce files suitable for Internet use. However, Paint Shop Pro makes it even easier to produce transparent GIF and JPEG files by providing specialised export dialogs.

Exporting GIF/JPEG files – the advanced route

1 Pull down the File menu and click Export

2 In the sub-menu, click Transparent Gif OR JPEG file

3 Complete the dialog which launches (the dialog below appears if you select Transparent Gif. Some of the JPEG file options are different):

 Repeat steps 4-5 for the appropriate tabs/options. Finally, perform step 6.

4 Activate the relevant tab

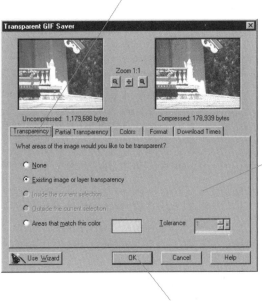

 Paint Shop Pro provides a simpler way to produce specialised GIF and JPEG files.

After step 2, click this button:

Now complete the dialogs which launch. (Click Next to move on to subsequent ones.) In the final dialog, click Finish.

5 Complete the associated options, as appropriate

6 Click here

File formats – an overview

The images Paint Shop Pro works with fall into three categories:

- bitmaps (also known as raster formats)

- vector images

- meta images

Many bitmap formats have compression as an option. This allows bitmaps – often very large – to be stored on disk in much smaller files.

Bitmap images

Bitmaps consist of pixels (dots) arranged in such a way that they form a graphic image. Because of the very nature of bitmaps, the question of 'resolution' – the sharpness of an image expressed in dpi (dots per inch) – is important. Bitmaps look best if they're displayed at their correct resolution. Paint Shop Pro imports (i.e. translates into its own format) a wide variety of third-party bitmap formats.

Once you've finished working with bitmaps, you can export the finished result as another bitmap. In this way, they can be utilised in other programs (e.g. CorelDRAW).

Paint Shop Pro will read 13 vector formats. However, it can only save to 5 vector formats (and even then, only bitmap information is written).

Vector images

Paint Shop Pro will also import vector graphics files in formats native to other programs. Vector images consist of, and are defined by, algebraic equations. One practical result of this is that they can be rescaled without any loss of definition. Another corollary is that they're less complex than bitmaps: they contain less detail.

Many vector formats (e.g. Encapsulated PostScript) can also incorporate bitmapped data, too, and therefore approach the functionality of meta formats.

Meta images

These are blanket formats which explicitly allow the inclusion of raster and vector data, as well as text annotations.

Brief notes on image formats

Another bitmap format – JPEG (Joint Photographic Experts Group) – is used for photograph storage, especially on the Internet. It supports a very high-level of compression, usually without appreciable distortion.

Another bitmap format now used increasingly on the Web is Interlaced Portable Network Graphics (suffix: .PNG).

An example of a meta format is Windows Metafile (suffix: .WMF). This can be used for data exchange between just about all Windows programs).

Paint Shop Pro will import a wide selection of bitmap, vector and meta graphic formats. These are some of the main ones:

Bitmap formats

PCX — Originated with PC Paintbrush. Used for years to transfer graphics data between Windows application. Supports compression

TIFF — Tagged Image File Format. Suffix: .TIF. If anything, even more widely used than PCX, across a whole range of platforms and applications

BMP — Not as common as PCX and TIFF, but still popular. Tends to produce large files

TGA — Targa. A high-end format, and also a bridge with so-called low-end computers (e.g. Amiga and Atari). Often used in PC and Mac paint and ray-tracing programs because of its high-resolution colour fidelity. Supports compression

GIF — Graphics Interchange Format. Just about any Windows program – and a lot more besides – will read GIF. Frequently used on the Internet. Disadvantage: it can't handle more than 256 colours. Compression is supported

PCD — (Kodak) PhotoCD. Used primarily to store photographs on CD. Paint Shop Pro will not export to PCD

Vector formats

CGM — Computer Graphics Metafile. Frequently used in the past, especially as a medium for clip-art transmission. Less frequently used nowadays

EPS — The most widely used PostScript format. Combines vector and raster data with a low-resolution informational bitmap header. The preferred vector format

Zoom

 Paint Shop Pro uses a simple nomenclature to denote what happens when you zoom in or out.

For example, an image at its normal view level is described as:

1:1

If you zoom in three times, this is shown as:

3:1

Alternatively, if you zoom out six times, this is shown as:

1:6

(You can zoom in to 32:1, and out to 1:24.)

The ability to 'zoom in' (magnify) or 'zoom out' (reduce magnification) is very important when you're working with images in Paint Shop Pro. When you zoom in or out, Paint Shop Pro increases or reduces the magnification by single increments.

1 Click this button in the Tool Palette:

2 Place the mouse pointer where you want to zoom in or out

 Re step 3 – you should repeat this as often as necessary.

3 Left-click to zoom in, OR right-click to zoom out

The result of zooming in

Full Screen Preview mode

Paint Shop Pro also has another view mode: **Full Screen Edit. This** hides:

- **the Title bar**
- **the Menu bar, and;**
- **the Status bar**

To launch (or leave) Full Screen Edit mode, press Shift+A.

Paint Shop Pro has a special screen mode which shows the current image (minus other screen components) set against a black background.

Use Full Screen Preview mode to preview changes you've made (and as a preliminary to running the more detailed Print Preview mode – see chapter 7).

Entering Full Screen Preview mode

Pull down the View menu and click Full Screen Preview.

An image in Full Edit mode

An image viewed normally

To leave Full Screen Preview, press Esc.

The same image in Full Screen Preview mode

Undo and Revert

You can undo more than one action at a time.

Ignore step 1 on the right. Instead, pull down the Edit menu and click Command History. Do the following:

A Click an undo level

B Click here

(Note that selecting a lower undo level automatically selects levels above it).

Paint Shop Pro has two features which, effectively, allow you to revert to the way things were *before* you carried out one or more amendments to the active image.

The Undo command

You can 'undo' (i.e. reverse) the last editing action by issuing a menu command.

Pull down the Edit menu and do the following:

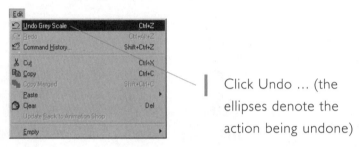

Click Undo ... (the ellipses denote the action being undone)

Repeat step 1 to undo subsequent actions.

The Revert command

You can – in a single command – undo *all* the editing changes made to an image since it was last saved. You do this by having Paint Shop Pro abandon the changes and reopen the last-saved file.

Pull down the File menu and do the following:

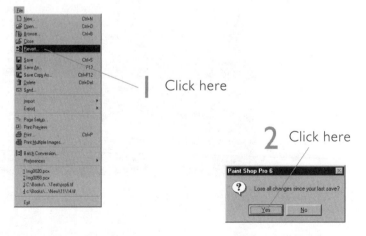

Click here

2 Click here

Redo

Paint Shop Pro also lets you undo undoes. This is called 'redoing' an action

The Redo command

You can 'undo' (i.e. reverse) the last editing action by issuing a menu command.

Pull down the Edit menu and do the following:

A Click a redo level

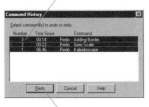

| Click Redo ... (the ellipses denote the action being undone)

B Click here

(Clicking a higher redo level automatically selects levels below it).

Redoing in action:

The Kaleidoscope effect has been applied and then 'undone'...

The result of 'redoing' it

Background/foreground colours

Paint Shop Pro uses two broad colour definitions (called 'active' colours):

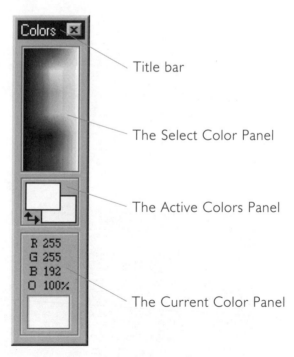

The Color Palette is normally fixed on the right of the screen. However, since Paint Shop Pro treats it as a toolbar it can, as here, have an independent existence (this is called 'floating').

To make the Color Palette float, double-click anywhere in the Select Color Panel (but outside the colours). Now drag the Color Palette to a new location.

To return the Color Palette to its default location (this is called 'docking'), double-click its Title bar.

Foreground colours — these occupy image foregrounds and are invoked with the left mouse button

Background colours — these occupy image backgrounds and are invoked with the right mouse button

The way you work with foreground and background colours is crucial to your use of Paint Shop Pro. Fortunately, selecting the appropriate colours – via the on-screen Color Palette – is very easy and straightforward.

The Color Palette defined

The Color Palette has the following sections:

Colors

Title bar

The Select Color Panel

The Active Colors Panel

R 255
G 255
B 192
O 100%

The Current Color Panel

...cont'd

Steps 3-4 apply if the active image has fewer than 16 million colours.

If you're working with images with 16 million colours or over, however, Paint Shop Pro launches the Color dialog after step 1 or 2 in 'Using the Active Colors Panel'. Omit steps 3 and 4. Instead, do the following:

A Drag on the colour ring to select a hue

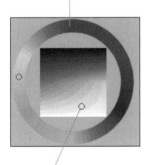

B Drag the selector to adjust the saturation

Finally, click OK.

Using the Select Color Panel

Move the mouse pointer over the Select Color Panel. The pointer changes to:

Move the pointer over the colours in the Select Color Panel; as you do so, the details in the Current Color Panel update automatically. When you find the colour you want to use, do ONE of the following:

1 Left-click once to select it as a foreground colour

2 Right-click once to select it as a background colour

Using the Active Colors Panel

You can use another method to select a foreground/background colour. Refer to the Active Colors Panel. Carry out steps 1, 3 and 4 below to select a foreground colour, OR 2-4 to pick a background colour:

1 Click here

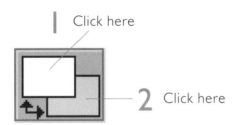

2 Click here

4 Click here

3 Click a colour

The Clear command

Paint Shop Pro does not copy the original image or image selection to the Windows Clipboard. If you need to restore the image, however, you can do so by using the Undo feature (see page 22).

You can have Paint Shop Pro automatically replace an image (or a selection within an image) with the current background colour.

Using Clear

1 Set the relevant background colour via the Color Palette (see pages 24-25)

2 Optional – define the appropriate selection area (see chapter 2 for how to do this)

3 Pull down the Edit menu and click Clear

Clearing in action:

If you perform steps 1-3 on a non-floating raster (bitmap) selection, the only effect is to delete the selection.
(On the other hand, steps 1-3 on a vector selection delete the vector object).
See chapter 2 for more information on selection types.

A selection area has been defined

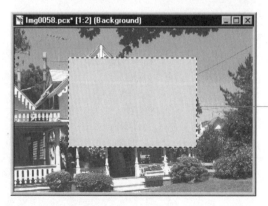

The selection area after a Clear operation

Clearing a selection area on a layer makes it transparent.

Making selections

In this chapter, you'll learn about selection types. You'll define rectangular, square, elliptical and circular bitmap selections, then select previously created vector objects. You'll also learn to deselect, invert and move selections, then amend selection feathering. Finally, you'll save selections for reuse later, and create multiple/subtractive selections.

Covers

Chapter Two

Selections – an overview

The types on the right are bitmap (raster) selections. However, you can also select vector objects you've created earlier – see page 38.

Selecting all or part of a Paint Shop Pro image is the essential preliminary for performing any of the many supported editing operations.

You can make the following kinds of selections:

- rectangular
- square
- elliptical
- circular
- freehand
- colour-based
- additive and subtractive

To select the whole of the active image in one go, simply press Ctrl+A. (This also selects vector objects.)

Additionally, you can select an entire image in one operation.

Once part of an image has been selected, you can perform the following, selection-specific operations:

— changing selection modes

— removing (deselecting) selections

— inverting bitmap selections

— moving parts of an image

— amending bitmap feathering (the degree of hardness with which the selection is drawn)

— specifying a transparent colour (as a means of limiting selections)

You can also save image selections to disk as special files, and then reopen them at will within other images.

Selection borders

Selected vector objects (see chapter 3 for how to create them) have unbroken borders interspersed with nodes e.g.:

An Edit node – see chapter 3

Generally, whenever you make a bitmap selection in Paint Shop Pro, you'll select *part* of an image. Whether you do this or select an image in its entirety, the portion you've selected is surrounded with a dotted line:

A magnified view of the selection border

A rectangular selection

The selection border (sometimes called a 'marquee') moves, which makes it very easy to locate.

Selection modes

To float a selection, press Ctrl+F.
To defloat a selection (return it to Standard), press Ctrl+Shift+F.

You can use two kinds of bitmap selection:

Standard — These form part of the original image. In other words, if you move a selection area (see pages 41-42), Paint Shop Pro fills the resultant gap with the background colour

Floating/ defloating does not apply to vector objects.

Floating — When a selection area is 'floating', the contents are deemed to be on top of (and distinct from) the original

Floating v. Standard selections:

If you float a selection on a vector layer (see chapter 7 for more information on layers), it is rasterised.

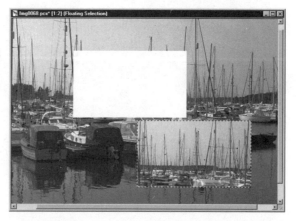

A Standard selection. The selection has been moved, filling the gap with the active background

If you hold down Alt as you drag a Standard selection, it is automatically floated.

A Floating selection. As above, but the underlying image is unaffected

Creating rectangular selections

You can create rectangular bitmap selections in two ways:

 If the Tool Options toolbar isn't on-screen, right-click the Tool Palette and select Tool Options in the menu.

- with the use of the mouse
- with the use of a special dialog

The mouse route

Ensure the Tool Palette is on-screen (if it isn't, right-click any toolbar – in the menu, select Tool Palette). Then do the following:

 Re step 2 – if the Tool Options toolbar is on-screen but only its Title bar displays:

move the mouse pointer over the Title bar to make the rest of the window appear.

Click here

2 Refer to the Tool Options toolbar and do the following:

3 Ensure this tab is active

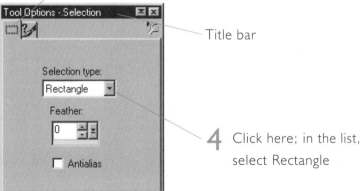

Title bar

 **To specify the amount of feathering (the sharpness of the selection), type in a value in the Feather: field. Note the following range:**
- **0 — maximum sharpness, and;**
- **200 — maximum softness**

4 Click here; in the list, select Rectangle

...cont'd

The Rectangle and Square selection cursor looks like this:

To create a square selection with the mouse, follow steps 1-3 on page 31. In step 4, select Square instead. Now carry out steps 5-7 on the right.

5 Place the mouse pointer at the corner of the area you want to select

6 Drag to define the selection

7 Release the mouse button when you've finished

The dialog route

Refer to the Tool Palette and do the following:

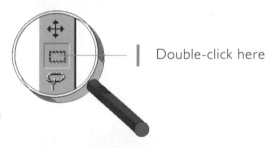

Double-click here

To create a square selection via a dialog, follow the steps on the right (in step 2, type in the appropriate pixel positions).

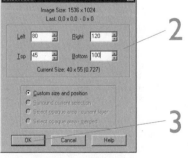

2 Type in the positions (in pixels) of the four corners

3 Click here

Creating elliptical selections

1 Perform steps 1-3 on page 31

2 In step 4 on page 31, select Ellipse

3 Place the mouse pointer at the corner of the area you want to select

 To create a circular selection, follow step 1 on the right. In step 2, however, select Circle. Now carry out steps 3-5.

Skyrides.jpg* [1:1] (Background)

4 Drag to define the selection

5 Release the mouse button when you've finished

Irregular selections

You can use a special Paint Shop Pro tool – the Freehand tool – to create selections by hand.

Creating freehand selections

Ensure the Tool Palette is on-screen (if it isn't, right-click any toolbar – in the menu, select Tool Palette). Then do the following:

| Click here

2 Refer to the Tool Options toolbar and do the following:

3 Ensure this tab is active

— Title bar

4 Click here; in the list, click Freehand

5 Type in a Feathering setting (in the range: 0-200)

...cont'd

The Freehand cursor looks like this:

You can contract bitmap selections uniformly (the shape is retained) via a dialog.

Pull down the Selections menu and click Modify, Contract. In the Number of pixels: field in the Contract Selection dialog, type in the extent of the contraction (in pixels). Click OK.

6 Place the mouse pointer at the location where you want the selection to begin

7 Drag to define the selection

8 Release the mouse button when you've finished

Selections based on colour

If the Tool Options toolbar isn't on-screen, right-click the Tool Palette and select Tool Options in the menu.

You can use another Paint Shop Pro tool – the Magic Wand – to select portions of the active image which share a specific colour.

Creating colour-based selections

Ensure the Tool Palette is on-screen (if it isn't, right-click any toolbar – in the menu, select Tool Palette). Then do the following:

Re step 2 – if the Tool Options toolbar is on-screen but only its Title bar displays:

Tool Options - Selection

move the mouse pointer over the Title bar to make the rest of the window appear.

| Click here

Type in a value in the Tolerance field. (Tolerance is the degree to which image pixels must approach the chosen one to activate selection.) Use this range:

- **0 — only exact matches result in selection, and;**
- **200 — all pixels are selected**

2 Refer to the Tool Options toolbar and do the following:

3 Ensure this tab is active

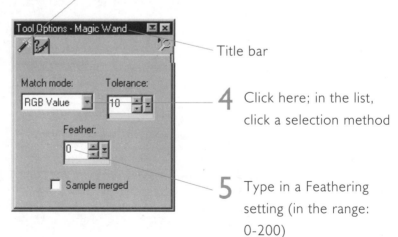

— Title bar

4 Click here; in the list, click a selection method

5 Type in a Feathering setting (in the range: 0-200)

...cont'd

 The Magic Wand cursor looks like this:

 You can expand bitmap selections uniformly (the shape is retained) via a dialog.

Pull down the Selections menu and click Modify, Expand. In the Number of pixels: field in the Expand Selection dialog, type in the extent of the expansion (in pixels). Click OK.

 To remove a specific colour from an existing selection, follow steps 1-5 on the facing page. Now hold down Ctrl as you click the colour.

6 Place the mouse pointer over the area you want to select

7 Left-click once

The end result:

The new selection area

Vector selections

To select vector objects you've already created, carry out the following procedure.

Selecting one or more vector objects

1 Refer to the Tool Palette and do the following:

See chapter 3 for how to create vector objects.

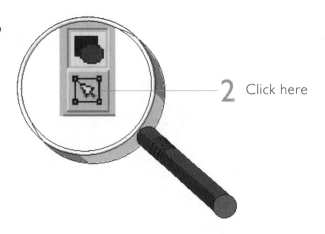

2 Click here

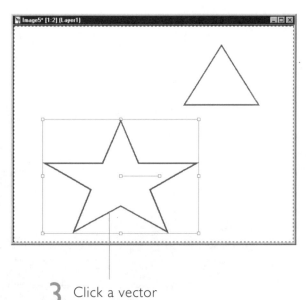

Re step 3 – to select more than one vector object, hold down Shift as you click them.

3 Click a vector object's outline

Deselecting selections

You can disable all selections you've already made in two ways:

Both procedures on the right work with raster selections.
However, to deselect all vector selections, press Ctrl+D instead. Alternatively, if this tool is active in the Tool Palette:

simply left-click outside a selection.

The menu route

Pull down the Selections menu and do the following:

Click here

The mouse route

Provided one of these Tool Palette tools is active:

you can do the following:

| Within the active image, right-click once

Inverting selections

When you've selected a portion of an image, you can have Paint Shop Pro do BOTH of the following:

When you invert freehand selections, Paint Shop Pro may not display the inversion accurately. However, any editing changes you make to the selected area will display correctly.

- deselect the selected area

- select the external area which was previously unselected

Paint Shop Pro calls this 'inverting a selection'. Use inversion as a means of creating selections which would otherwise be difficult – or impossible – to achieve.

Inverting a selection

First make a normal selection. Then pull down the Selections menu and click Invert.

Inversion in action:

In the lower figure, Paint Shop Pro has also surrounded the selected area (here, the image minus the additive selection) with a dotted border:

An additive selection (see page 47)

After inversion – the dotted border now encloses the *unselected* area

Moving selections

To move a vector object, ensure this Tool Palette tool is active:

Now click the object's outline. Keep the pointer on the outline until it looks like this:

Hold down the left mouse button and drag the object to a new location. Release the mouse button.

Ensure the selection frame has not been made floating (see page 30) before carrying out the procedures here.

Paint Shop Pro lets you move bitmap selection areas. You can:

• move just the frame which defines the selection area

OR

• move the frame AND the contents

Moving selection frames only

Refer to the Tool Palette and do the following:

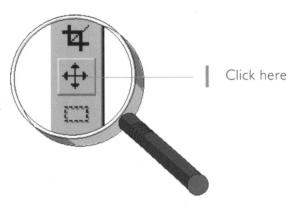

Click here

2 Right-click inside the existing selection area, then drag it to a new location

Moving selection frames in action:

The irregular selection area from the facing page has been moved

...cont'd

You can also move selections and their contents with the keyboard.

Hold down Shift. Now press and hold down any of the cursor keys.

(Hold down Ctrl as well as Shift to increase the move speed.)

Moving bitmap selection frames and contents

First, ensure that the selection area is Standard or Floating, according to the effect you want to achieve. (See page 30 for a description of the two possible effects). Then do the following:

1   In the Tool Palette, activate the tool which was used to create the selection

2   Drag the selection to a new location

Moving selection contents in action:

The procedures in the above tip also apply to selected vector objects (except that the underlying image is unaffected).

Moving the contents of a Standard selection

When you move a Standard selection, the original area is filled with the active background colour.

Moving the contents of a Floating selection

Amending selection feathering

As we've seen, when you define a selection within an image, you have the opportunity to customise the feathering. However, you can also do this (and to a greater extent) *after* the selection area has been created.

Re step 1 – **feathering** **refers to** **the** **sharpness of the** **selection. Note the** **following range:**
- **0 — maximum** **sharpness, and;**
- **200 — maximum** **softness**

Imposing a new feathering

Define a selection. Pull down the Selections menu and click Modify, Feather. Now do the following:

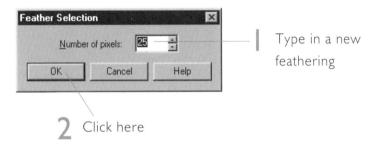

Type in a new feathering

2 Click here

Re-featuring in action:

A magnified view of the feathered selection edge

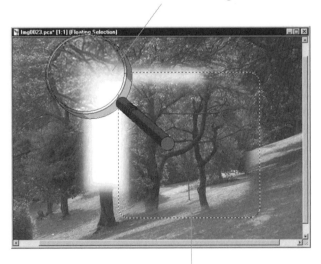

This square selection has been dragged to the right

Selecting a transparent colour

Re. step 1 – the Remove Selected Color dialog only lets you select a few basic colours.

For more precision, though, follow the procedures on page 25 to select a specific background or foreground colour, then select Foreground Color or Background Color.

Finally, follow step 2.

You can specify a transparent colour; this tells Paint Shop Pro to deselect it within a selection.

Selecting a colour

Define a selection. Pull down the Selections menu and click Modify, Transparent Color. Now do the following:

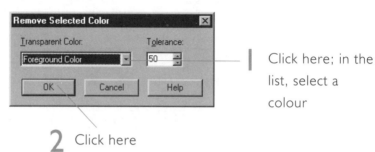

Click here; in the list, select a colour

2 Click here

Transparent colour selection in action:

In this example, a rectangular selection was made around the turret, then one of the turret colours was selected as the Foreground colour (with a fairly low tolerance). In step 1, Foreground Color was selected. Then, when the frame was moved to the left, all colours apart from the foreground were moved.

Moving this selection area illustrates transparent colour selection – see the DON'T FORGET tip

Reusing selections

Re transparent colour selection on the facing page – also type in a value in the Tolerance field. (Tolerance is the degree to which image pixels must approach the chosen one to activate selection.) Use this range:

- **0 — only exact matches result in selection, and;**
- **200 — all pixels are selected**

Paint Shop Pro lets you save a selection area (the frame, NOT the contents) to disk, as a special file. You can then load it into a new image. This is a convenient way to reuse complex selections.

An unusual selection, saved to disk...

See pages 47-48 for how to create selections like this.

... and then loaded into another image

...cont'd

Selection files have the following suffix: .SEL

Saving a selection

Define a selection. Pull down the Selections menu and click Save To Disk. Now do the following:

Click here; in the drop-down list, select a drive

Re step 1 – you may also have to double-click one or more folders first, to locate the folder you want to save the selection to.

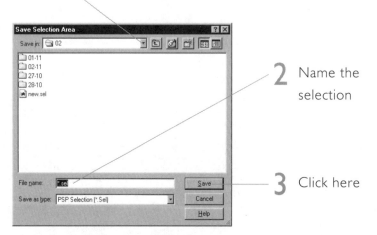

2 Name the selection

3 Click here

Loading a selection

Pull down the Selections menu and click Load From Disk. Now do the following:

Re step 1 – you may also have to double-click one or more folders first, to locate the folder which hosts the relevant selection file.

Click here; in the drop-down list, select a drive

2 Double-click a selection

Selection additions/subtractions

When you create multiple selections, a plus sign is added to the cursor for the relevant tool. For example, the Rectangle selector looks like this:

You can define *multiple* (additive) selections. This is a very useful technique which enables you to create spectacular effects. You can also create selections subtractively, where Paint Shop Pro decreases the size of a selection in line with further contiguous selections you define.

Creating multiple selections

1 Define the first selection, using any of the techniques previously discussed:

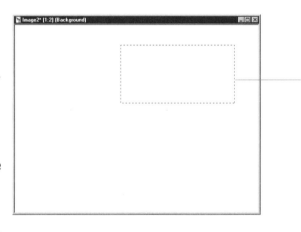

Here, a rectangular selection has been created

Re step 2 – if (as here) you define a further selection which encroaches onto the first, the two are joined.
If, on the other hand, you define the second selection so that it does not touch the first, this creates two separate selections:

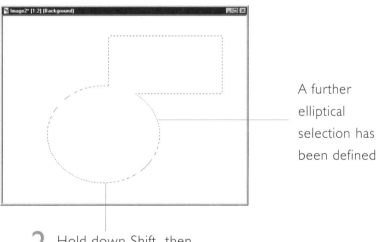

A further elliptical selection has been defined

Two independent selections

2 Hold down Shift, then define another selection

Creating subtractive selections

Define the first selection, using any of the techniques previously discussed:

When you perform selection subtract-ions, Paint Shop Pro adds a minus sign to the cursor for the relevant selection tool. For example, the Rectangle selector looks like this:

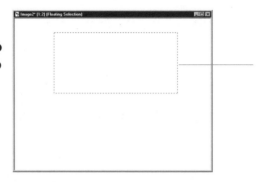

Here, a rectangular selection has been created

Re step 2 on page 47 – if you're using the Magic Wand to create multiple selections, simply hold down Shift as you click the area you want to add.

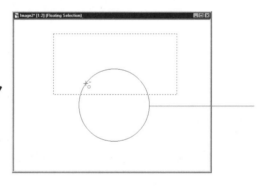

2 Hold down Ctrl as you define another contiguous selection

3 Release the mouse button

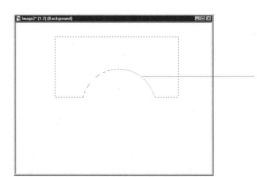

Paint Shop Pro has 'subtracted' the second selection from the first

Painting and drawing

In this chapter, you'll learn how to create a variety of painting/drawing effects. You'll perform freehand painting; copy colours; carry out colour substitutions; select specific colours for foreground/background use; retouch images; carry out spray painting; fill images with colours, other images ('patterns') and gradients; and paint with object collections (picture tubes). Finally, you'll format and insert text; create lines and preset shapes; then reshape them by moving their nodes.

Covers

Chapter Three

Painting and drawing – an overview

Re step 4 on the facing page – use these guidelines:

- **Shape — select a shape (e.g. Square or Horizontal)**
- **Size — select a brush size in pixels (in the range 1-255)**
- **Hardness — select a % in the range 0-100**
- **Opacity — select a % in the range 1-100 (100 is maximum opacity)**
- **Step (mimics brush contact) — select a % in the range 1-100**
- **Density — select a % in the range 1-100**

With many of the operations in this chapter (e.g. fills and picture tubes), you can restrict the effect to specific parts of an image by using selection areas or masks.

Paint Shop Pro lets you paint and draw on-screen, using a variety of specialised but easy to use tools located within the Tools Palette.

You can:

- create freehand paintings/drawings
- copy colours within images
- carry out colour substitutions (globally and manually)
- select existing colours as active foreground or background colours
- carry out image retouching (the manual application of special effects to images or image selections)
- carry out spray painting/drawing
- fill images with colours
- fill images with patterns (other open images)
- fill images with gradients
- format and insert raster or vector text into images
- edit existing vector text
- apply vector text onto vector object outlines
- create single, freehand and Bezier lines/curves
- create preset shapes (circles, ellipses, squares, rectangles, triangles etc.)
- reshape vector objects by dragging their nodes (you can also create your own nodes)
- paint with object collections (called 'picture tubes')

Painting with the Paintbrush tool

If the Tool Options toolbar isn't on-screen, right-click the Tool Palette and select Tool Options in the menu.

Creating a painting

Refer to the Tool Palette and do the following:

Click here

To apply a paper texture, click this tab:

Now click in the Paper texture: field. In the list, select a texture.

2 Refer to the Tool Options toolbar and do the following:

3 Ensure this tab is active

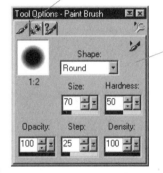

4 Complete these fields (see the HOT TIP on the facing page)

Re step 6 – carry out one of the following:

- **drag with the left mouse button to paint with the active foreground colour (see page 25), or;**
- **drag with the right mouse button to paint with the active background colour**

5 Place the mouse pointer where you want to start painting

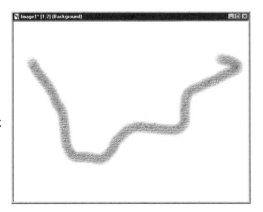

6 Define the painting, then release the mouse button

Drawing with the Paintbrush tool

Drawing lines

Refer to the Tool Palette and do the following:

| Click here

You can also use the Draw tool to draw lines – see pages 78-79.

2 Complete steps 2-4 on page 51

3 Click where you want the first line segment to begin

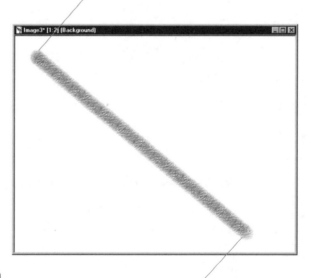

Repeat step 4 to define any further line segments which are required.

4 Hold down Shift, then click where you want the first segment to end

Copying with the Clone brush

Cloning is the copying of colour from one location within an image to another (or to another image which has the same number of colours). To clone colours, you use the Clone brush.

Cloning

Refer to the Tool Palette and do the following:

Click here

 Re step 4 – use the following as guidelines:

- **Shape — select a shape (e.g. Square or Horizontal)**
- **Size — select a brush size in pixels (in the range 1-255)**
- **Hardness — select a % in the range 0-100**
- **Opacity — select a % in the range 1-100 (100 = maximum opacity)**
- **Step (mimics brush contact) — select a % in the range 1-100**
- **Density — select a % in the range 1-100**

2 Refer to the Tool Options toolbar and do the following:

3 Ensure this tab is active

4 Complete these fields

5 Carry out the additional steps on page 54

6 Place the mouse pointer over the image section you want to copy

7 Right-click once

The Clone crosshairs indicate the pixel which is currently being copied. As you drag in step 8, the crosshairs move, so you can select (on-the-fly) the area being copied.

8 Position the cursor where you want the paste operation to take place, then drag repeatedly

Magnified view of crosshairs

Replacing colours globally

You can have Paint Shop Pro replace a specified colour with another. You do this by nominating the colour you want to replace as the foreground colour, then selecting the new colour as the background colour. (Or vice versa).

You can replace colours:

* globally (within the whole of an image, or a selection area)

* manually (by using the Color Replacer tool as a brush)

Carrying out a global substitution
Refer to the Tool Palette and do the following:

| Click here

Re step 4 on the facing page – use these guidelines:

* **Shape — select a shape (e.g. Square or Horizontal)**
* **Size — select a brush size in pixels (in the range 1-255)**
* **Step (mimics brush contact) — select a % in the range 1-100**
* **Density — select a % in the range 1-100**

2 Refer to the Tool Options toolbar and do the following:

3 Ensure this tab is active

4 Complete these fields

5 Carry out the additional steps on page 56

6 Optional – if you want to limit the colour exchange to a selected area, define the relevant area now

7 Carry out step 8 OR 9 below:

8 Double-click the left mouse button to replace the background with the foreground colour

9 Double-click the right mouse button to replace the foreground with the background colour

The end result:

Here, the colour in the saucer has been replaced with white...

Replacing colours manually

Carrying out a manual substitution
Refer to the Tool Palette and do the following:

Replacing colours manually requires a light touch (and experimentation with the available settings – see step 2).

| Click here

Re step 3 – carry out ONE of the following:

- **drag with the left mouse button to replace the background with the foreground colour, or;**
- **drag with the right mouse button to replace the foreground with the background colour**

2 Complete steps 2-4 on page 55

3 Drag over the relevant area to carry out the substitution – see the DON'T FORGET tip

4 Release the mouse button when you've finished

Replacing colours with lines

Replacing colours with lines requires a light touch (and experimentation with the available settings).

The Color Replacer tool also lets you substitute colours as you create lines.

Replacing colours while drawing lines

Refer to the Tool Palette and do the following:

Click here

Re steps 3-4 – carry out one of the following:

• **click with the left mouse button to replace the background with the foreground colour, or;**
• **click with the right mouse button to replace the foreground with the background colour**

2 Complete steps 2-4 on page 55

3 Click where you want the line to start

Here, the roof is being replaced with white.

Repeat step 4 as often as necessary.

4 To create a line segment, hold down Shift and click elsewhere

Using the Dropper tool

You can activate the Dropper (within most paint tools) by holding down one Ctrl key.

The Dropper is an extremely useful tool which you can use to:

1. select a colour in the active image

2. nominate this as the active foreground or background colour

Using the Dropper

Refer to the Tool Palette and do the following:

Re step 2 – carry out one of the following:

*   **click with the left mouse button to nominate the selected colour as the foreground, or;**
*   **click with the right mouse button to nominate the selected colour as the background**

Click here

After step 2, the selected colour appears in the Color Palette:

The new foreground colour

2 Click a colour – see the DON'T FORGET tip

Retouching – an overview

Paint Shop Pro also provides retouch operations which work specifically with colour e.g.:

- **Saturation Up, and;**
- **Saturation Down**

which increase/ decrease colour saturation respectively.

You can't perform retouching operations globally.
  However, there are three exceptions to this:

- **Embossing**
- **Softening, and;**
- **Sharpening**

  You can apply a special filter to achieve these effects:

- **on the whole of an image, or;**
- **on a specific selection area**

  See chapter 4 for more information.

You can use the Retouch tool to perform photo-retouching operations on images (or selected areas within images).

These operations include:

Lighten RGB	makes the image or selection brighter
Darken RGB	makes the image or selection darker
Soften	mutes the image or selection and diminishes contrast
Sharpen	emphasises edges and accentuates contrast
Emboss	produces a raised ('stamped') effect (where the foreground is emphasised in relation to the background)
Smudge	produces a stained, blurred effect
Push	like Smudge but no colour is picked up
Dodge	lightens image shadow
Burn	darkens images

All the above tools (excluding Dodge and Burn) work with images which are 24 bit (16 million colours) or greyscale; the remainder work only with 24 bit images.

Ways to use the Retouch tool
You can use the Retouch tool:

— as a brush

— to draw lines

Retouching images manually

Carrying out a manual retouch operation

Refer to the Tool Palette and do the following:

Retouching images manually requires a light touch (and experimentation with the available settings – see step 2).

Click here

After step 2, to select a retouch operation click this tab in the Tool Options toolbar:

Now click in the Retouch mode: field. In the list, select an operation.
Also, click in the Paper texture: field. In the list, select a texture.

2 Complete steps 2-4 on page 55, as appropriate

3 Hold down the left mouse button and drag over the relevant area

Here, an Emboss retouching operation is being carried out.

4 Release the mouse button when you've finished

Retouching images with lines

To retouch images by defining lines, carry out the procedures described below.

Retouching images while drawing lines
Refer to the Tool Palette and do the following:

| Click here

Re step 4 – for how to complete these fields, see the HOT TIP on page 50.

2 Refer to the Tool Options toolbar and do the following:

After step 4, to select a retouch operation click this tab in the Tool Options toolbar:

3 Ensure this tab is active

4 Complete these fields, as appropriate

Now click in the Retouch mode: field. In the list, select an operation.
Optionally, Also click in the Paper texture: field. In the list, select a texture.

5 Carry out the additional steps on the facing page

...cont'd

6 Click where you want the
retouch operation to begin

 **Here, a
Burn
retouching
operation
is being carried out.**

 **Repeat
step 7 for
as many
extra line
segments as you
want to insert.**

7 Hold down Shift and click where
you want the line segment to end

Painting with the Airbrush

You can use the Airbrush tool to simulate painting with a spray can. You can do this in two ways:

- while using the Airbrush as a brush

- while using the Airbrush to draw lines

You can also select and apply a brush type. After step 3, click this button in the Tool Options toolbar:

In the menu, select a brush (e.g. Paintbrush or Charcoal). (Alternatively, click Custom in the menu. In the Custom Brush dialog, click a brush. Finally, click OK.)

Using the Airbrush as a brush

Refer to the Tool Palette and do the following:

Click here

2 Refer to the Tool Options toolbar and do the following:

3 Ensure this tab is active

After step 4, to select a paper texture, click this tab:

Now click in the Paper texture: field. In the list, select a texture.

4 Complete these fields, as appropriate (see the HOT TIP on page 50)

5 Carry out the additional steps on the facing page

...cont'd

6 Carry out step 7 OR 8 below:

7 Hold down the left mouse button, then drag to paint with the active foreground colour

 Here, the Shape setting (see step 4 on the facing page) has been set to Left Slash.

Img0034.pcx* [1:1] (Background)

8 Hold down the right mouse button, then drag to paint with the active background colour

9 Release the mouse button

Drawing with the Airbrush

Using the Airbrush to draw lines

Refer to the Tool Palette and do the following:

 You can also select and apply a brush type. After step 3, click this button in the Tool Options toolbar:

In the menu, select a brush (e.g. Paintbrush or Charcoal). (Alternatively, click Custom in the menu. In the Custom Brush dialog, click a brush. Finally, click OK.)

| Click here

2 Refer to the Tool Options toolbar and do the following:

3 Ensure this tab is active

4 Complete these fields, as appropriate (see the HOT TIP on page 50)

 After step 4, to select a paper texture, click this tab:

Now click in the Paper texture: field; in the list, select a texture.

5 Carry out the additional steps on the facing page

...cont'd

6 Click where you want the
retouch operation to begin

 **Here, a
custom
brush has
been
applied – see the
HOT TIP on the
facing page.**

 **Repeat
step 7 for
as many
extra line
segments as you
want to insert.**

7 Hold down Shift and click where
you want the line segment to end

Inserting colours with the Fill tool

You can use the Fill tool to

- fill an image with colour

- fill an image with a specific pattern (Paint Shop Pro defines 'patterns' as images you've already opened into additional windows)

- fill an image with a gradient (Paint Shop Pro supports 4 kinds: Linear, Rectangular, Sunburst, Radial)

Re step 5 – use the following as guidelines:

- **Blend mode — all options except Normal ensure that the fill is affected by the underlying image colours**
- **Paper texture — optionally, select a texture**
- **Match mode — select the method by which Paint Shop Pro decides which pixels are covered (None covers all pixels)**
- **Opacity — select a % in the range 1-100 (100 is maximum opacity), and;**
- **Tolerance — enter a value in this range: 0 (only exact matches are filled) to 200 (every pixel is filled)**

Filling images with a colour

Refer to the Tool Palette and do the following:

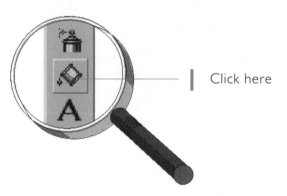

1 Click here

2 Refer to the Tool Options toolbar and do the following:

3 Ensure this tab is active

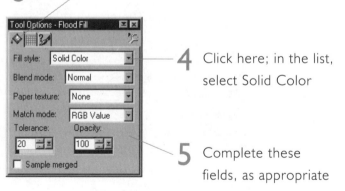

4 Click here; in the list, select Solid Color

5 Complete these fields, as appropriate

6 Carry out the additional steps on the facing page

...cont'd

If you want to limit the fill to a selection area, define it before step 1 on the facing page.

7 Left-click to insert the foreground colour, OR right-click to insert the background colour

A completed colour fill:

Inserting patterns with the Fill tool

 If you want to limit the fill to a selection area, define it before step 1.

Filling images with a pattern

First, open:

1.   the image you want to insert as a pattern

2.   the image into which you want to insert the pattern

Now refer to the Tool Palette and do the following:

 Re step 5 – for how to complete the fields in the Tool Options toolbar, see the DON'T FORGET tip on page 68.

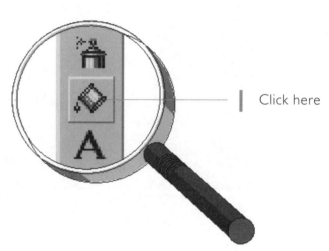

| Click here

 After step 5, click this button in the Tool Options toolbar:

Click in the New pattern source: field. In the list, select the active image you want to insert as a pattern.
Now carry out steps 6-7.

2 Refer to the Tool Options toolbar and do the following:

3 Ensure this tab is active

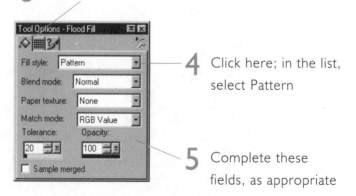

4 Click here; in the list, select Pattern

5 Complete these fields, as appropriate

6 Carry out the additional steps on the facing page

...cont'd

Images you apply pattern fills to must be:

- **24 bit (16 million colours), or;**
- **greyscale**

7 If the image into which you want to paste the pattern fill isn't already active, activate it now (by pressing Ctrl+F6 as often as required)

8 Left-click where you want the pattern fill inserted

A completed pattern fill:

Inserting gradients with the Fill tool

If you want to limit the fill to a selection area, define it before step 1.

Filling images with a gradient

Refer to the Tool Palette and do the following:

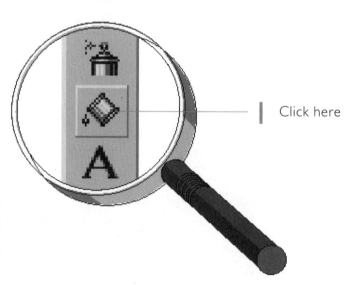

Click here

Re step 5 – for how to complete the fields in the Tool Options toolbar, see the DON'T FORGET tip on page 68.

After step 5, click this button in the Tool Options toolbar:

Click in the Gradient: field. In the list, select a gradient type (e.g. Metallic). Complete the rest of the fields (e.g. if you selected Linear Gradient in step 4, specify the gradient angle in the Angle: field).
Now carry out steps 6-7.

2 Refer to the Tool Options toolbar and do the following:

3 Ensure this tab is active

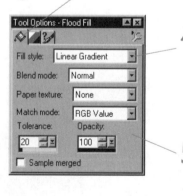

4 Click here; in the list, select Linear Gradient, Rectangular Gradient, Sunburst Gradient or Radial Gradient

5 Complete these fields, as appropriate

6 Carry out the additional steps on the facing page

...cont'd

7 Left- or right-click once (but see the DON'T FORGET tip)

Note that left-clicking defines a gradient from the foreground to the background colour, while right-clicking defines from the background to the foreground colour.

Non-linear gradient types:

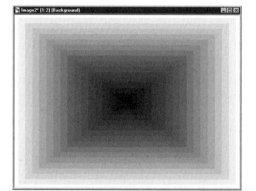

A Rectangular gradient

Images you apply gradient fills to must be:

- **24 bit (16 million colours), or;**
- **greyscale**

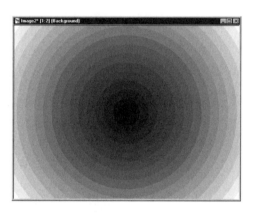

A Sunburst gradient

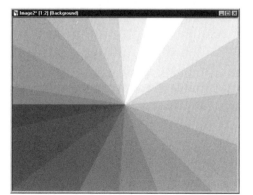

A Radial gradient

Inserting text with the Text tool

Paint Shop Pro lets you insert text into images, easily and conveniently. You can insert two principal types of text:

You can also create Selection (raster) text. Selection text is an empty, transparent selection e.g.:

Once created, Selection text can be edited with Paint Shop Pro's tools. In the following example, a different gradient fill has been applied to each letter:

Floating	Floating text appears above the current layer
Vector	You can only create vector text on a vector layer. Vector text is actually a vector object; as a result, it can be edited, moved and deformed. (It can also be added to paths.)

When you create text, you can specify:

1. a typeface and/or type size

2. a style. With most typefaces, you can choose from:

    — Regular

    — *Italic*

    — **Bold**

3. the following text effects

    — ~~Strikethrough~~

    — <u>Underline</u>

4. an alignment. You can choose from:

    — Left

    — Center

    — Right

Anti-aliasing is the process of removing jagged distortions; it makes text look and print smoother.

You can also elect to have Paint Shop Pro 'anti-alias' the text.

...cont'd

You can insert vector text onto vector object outlines.

With the Text tool active in the Tool Palette, move the mouse pointer over the relevant vector object until the cursor changes:

The new cursor

Now click the vector object. Complete the Text Entry dialog in line with steps 4-9 on page 76 (ensure Vector is selected in step 6).

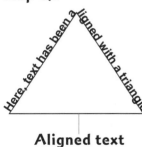

Aligned text

Inserting text
Refer to the Tool Palette and do the following:

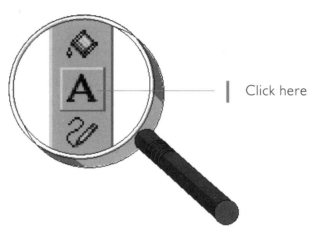

Click here

2 Place the mouse pointer where you want the text inserted

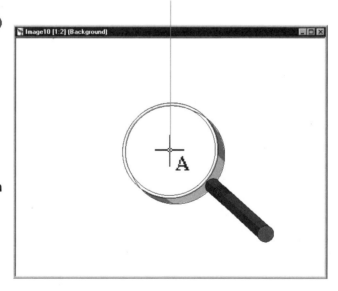

3 Left-click once

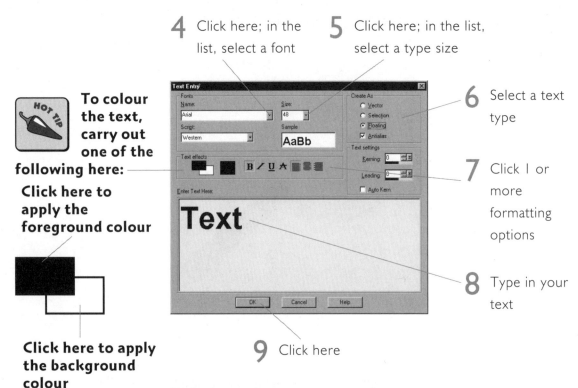

4 Click here; in the list, select a font

5 Click here; in the list, select a type size

6 Select a text type

7 Click 1 or more formatting options

8 Type in your text

9 Click here

To colour the text, carry out one of the following here:

Click here to apply the foreground colour

Click here to apply the background colour

Text in action:

Editing text

Paint Shop Pro lets you edit inserted vector text. Do the following:

You can only edit raster text in a limited way. For instance, you can:

- **apply fills with the paint tools, or;**
- **replace the text colour with the active background colour**

using standard selection editing techniques.

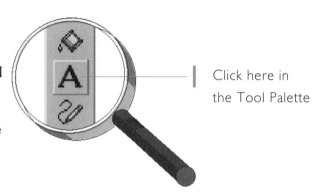

Click here in the Tool Palette

2 Place the mouse pointer over the text and left-click

3 Carry out steps 4-7 (as appropriate) on the facing page

4 Carry out step 8 on the facing page (but amend the existing text as appropriate)

5 Carry out step 9 on the facing page

Drawing with the Draw tool

After step 1, click this tab in the Tool Options toolbar:

Now click in the Type: field. In the list, select Single Line. Also, click in the Style: field and select a style in the list.

Finally, enter a line width in the Width: field (in the range 1-255) and – if required – select Create as vector.

Paint Shop Pro has a separate tool which you can use to create more detailed lines/curves.

You can draw:

- Single lines

- Freehand lines

- Bezier curves

You can create lines/curves as rasters or vectors (vectors are much more editable).

Drawing Single lines

Refer to the Tool Palette and do the following:

Click here

To define more segments, also carry out these steps:

4 Hold down Alt and click

5 Move the pointer to where you want the next segment to end and click. (Repeat as often as required)

6 Finally, release Alt and click again

2 Place the mouse pointer where you want the line to start

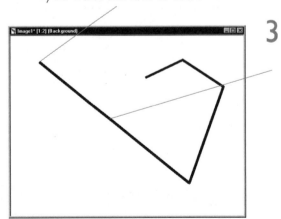

3 Drag with the left mouse button to draw with the foreground colour, or with the right to draw with the background colour

Drawing Freehand lines

Refer to the Tool Palette and do the following:

1 Click here

2 Refer to the Tool Options toolbar and do the following:

3 Ensure this tab is active

 Select Create as vector to define a vector Freehand line, or deselect this to create a raster line.

4 Click here; in the list, select Freehand Line

5 Complete the remaining fields, as appropriate

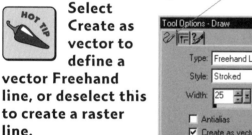 **Here, a vector Freehand line has been defined.**

 After step 6, release the mouse button.

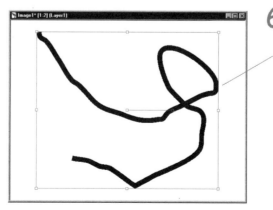

6 Drag with the left mouse button to draw with the foreground colour, or with the right to draw with the background colour

Drawing Bezier curves
Refer to the Tool Palette and do the following:

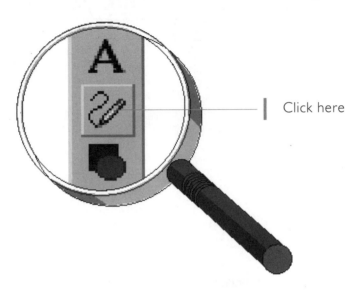

I Click here

2 Refer to the Tool Options toolbar and do the following:

3 Ensure this tab is active

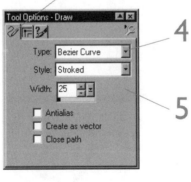

4 Click here; in the list, select Bezier Curve

5 Complete the remaining fields, as appropriate

Select Create as vector to define a vector Freehand line, or deselect this to create a raster line.

6 Carry out the additional steps on the facing page

7 Place the mouse pointer where you want the curve to start

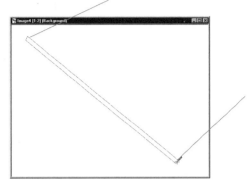

8 Drag with the left mouse button to draw with the foreground colour, or with the right to draw with the background colour

9 Click away from the start point to set the start target angle

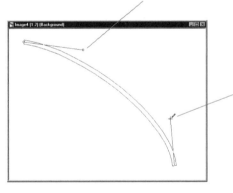

10 Click away from the end point to set the end target angle

The end result:

Here, a raster curve has been defined.

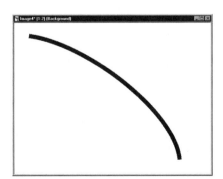

Using the Picture Tube tool

You can also paint using object collections called 'picture tubes'. When you do this, Paint Shop Pro automatically inserts a variety of related objects. For instance, if you paint with the Fish picture tube, a dozen different fish types are inserted...

Painting with the Picture Tube tool

Refer to the Tool Palette and do the following:

Re step 5 – complete the following fields:

- **Scale — set the tube size (in the range 10%-250%)**
- **Placement mode — select Random (objects appear at random intervals) or Continuous (objects are inserted at equal intervals), and;**
- **Selection mode — select Random (objects are chosen haphazardly); Incremental (objects are inserted one at a time); Angular (objects appear according to painting direction); or Velocity (objects appear according to painting speed)**

| Click here

2 Refer to the Tool Options toolbar and do the following:

3 Ensure this tab is active

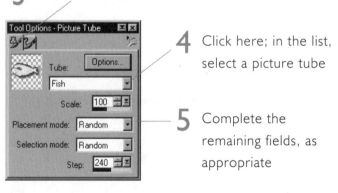

4 Click here; in the list, select a picture tube

5 Complete the remaining fields, as appropriate

6 Carry out the additional steps on the facing page

7 Place the mouse pointer where you want the tube to start

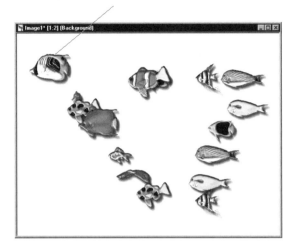

8 Drag with the left mouse button, then release it

Another picture tube:

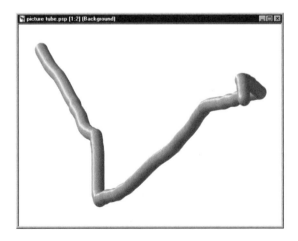

The 3D
Gold
picture tube

Drawing with the Preset Shapes tool

To edit vector shapes/ objects, click this button in the Tool Palette:

Now double-click the shape. The Vector Properties dialog launches; complete this as required. (For instance, to amend the shape width, type a new entry in the Width: field...) Finally, click OK.

You can create shapes (e.g. arrows, circles and stars).

Using the Preset Shapes tool
Refer to the Tool Palette and do the following:

1 Click here

2 Refer to the Tool Options toolbar and do the following:

3 Ensure this tab is active

Select Create as vector to define a vector shape, or deselect this to create a raster one.

4 Click here; in the list, select a shape (e.g. Triangle)

5 Complete the remaining fields, as appropriate

Here, a vector triangle has been defined.

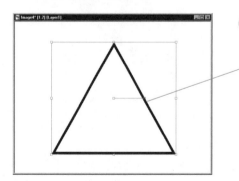

6 Drag with the left mouse button to draw with the foreground colour, or with the right to draw with the background colour

Node editing

 Paint Shop Pro has the following node types:

In Paint Shop Pro, vector objects contain nodes:

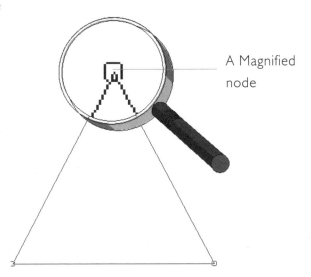

A Magnified node

- **Tangent — allows curves and lines to blend invisibly**
- **Corner (or Cusp) — apart from dragging the node (see page 86), you can also drag the node handles independently:**

Handles

- **Curve — produces very smooth curves**

You can use nodes to reshape objects in an almost infinite number of ways.

In the example below, the triangle in the above illustration has had its left node dragged inwards:

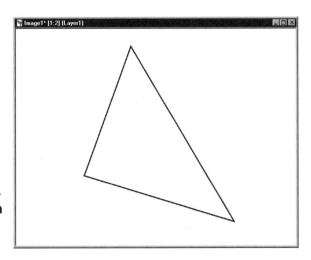

 To apply a new node type, right-click a node. In the menu, select Node Type. In the sub-menu, select the relevant option.

...cont'd

To add new nodes to vector objects, follow steps 1-5. Press Ctrl+D. Now hold down Ctrl as you click the object segment where you want the new node to appear. When the cursor changes to:

+ ADD

left-click once.

Warping vector objects with nodes:

1. Refer to the Tool Palette and do the following:

2. Click here

3. Click the outline of the relevant vector object

4. Right-click once – in the menu, select Node Edit

5. Right-click again – in the menu, select Drawing Mode

6. Left-click the relevant node

Re step 6 – to select multiple nodes, hold down Shift as you click them.

7. Drag the shape in or out, then release the mouse button

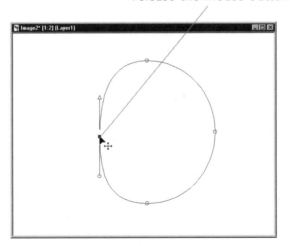

Re step 7 – to warp in 45° increm-ents, hold down Shift as you drag.

After you've finished warping the object, press Ctrl+Q.

Using filters

In this chapter, you'll learn how to add a variety of creative effects to images (or image selections). You'll do this by applying any of Paint Shop Pro's numerous filters. Finally, you'll create your own filters; amend user-defined filters; and apply these to images or image selections.

Covers

Chapter Four

Filters – an overview

Filters can be regarded as mini-programs built into Paint Shop Pro which alter the characteristics of individual pixels based on the relationship between:

- **the current colour, and;**
- **neighbouring colours**

Paint Shop Pro provides numerous special filters which you can use to customise images.

You can use filters to:

Enhance image edges

These include:

— Edge Enhance
— Edge Enhance More
— Find Edges
— Find Horizontal Edges
— Find Vertical Edges
— Trace Contour

Experiment with applying more than one filter to images (or the same filter more than once) – the effects can be dramatic.

Blur/sharpen images

These include:

— Blur
— Gaussian Blur
— Motion Blur
— Blur More
— Soften
— Soften More
— Sharpen
— Sharpen More
— Unsharpen

You can also create and apply your own filters.

Apply miscellaneous effects

These include:

— Add Noise
— Despeckle
— Dilate
— Emboss
— Erode
— Median Cut
— Mosaic
— Hot Wax

...cont'd

Filters only work with the following image types:

- **coloured images with more than 256 colours, and;**
- **256-colour greyscales**

If the image you want to apply a filter to doesn't meet the criteria in the above tip, press Ctrl+Shift+O to increase the colour depth to 16 million. (The 'O' in the above is zero.)

You can apply filters in two ways:

- via a menu

- via the Filter Browser

Both techniques are easy and convenient to use, but for most filters (where there is no intermediary dialog which allows you to specify filter settings), the Filter Browser is especially useful.

The Filter Browser

The Filter Browser is a special dialog which lets you preview the effects of applying a filter *before* you commit yourself to doing so.

It's also a way of accessing *every* available filter, without having to pull down a succession of menus.

In the following illustration, the Filter Browser is previewing the effect of applying the Trace Contour filter:

Filter effects are previewed here

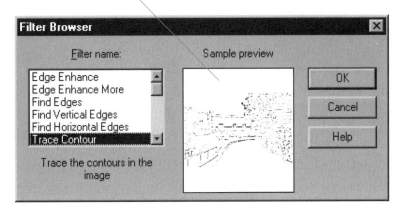

The Edge Enhance filter

Use the Edge Enhance filter to increase image clarity.

The illustration below shows an image *before* the Edge Enhance filter has been applied:

The Edge Enhance filter works by amplifying edge contrast.

You can also use the Edge Enhance More filter to achieve an even more marked effect:

(See the DON'T FORGET tips on the facing page.)

And now the result of applying the filter:

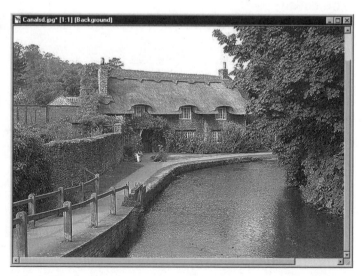

Using the Edge Enhance filter

Use either of the following methods to launch the Edge Enhance filter:

If you only want to apply the filter to a part of the image, define the appropriate selection area first.

The menu route
Pull down the Image menu and do the following:

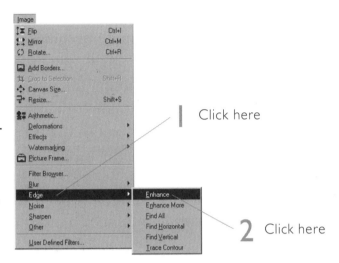

Click here

2 Click here

Re step 2 – to apply the Edge Enhance More filter instead, select Edge Enhance More.

The Browser route
Pull down the Image menu and click Filter Browser. Now do the following:

Re step 1 – to apply the Edge Enhance More filter instead, select Edge Enhance More.

Click Edge Enhance

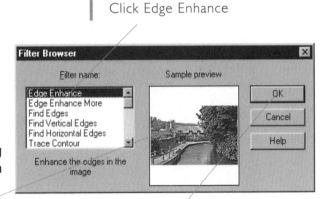

The effect of applying the chosen filter is previewed here:

2 Click here

The Find Edges filter

The Find Edges filter works by darkening an image and then emphasising all its edges.

Use the Find Edges filter when you need to identify – and emphasise – those parts of an image which have significant colour transitions.

The illustration below shows an image *before* the filter has been applied:

And now the result of applying the filter:

The Find Edges filter produces results which are dramatically creative.

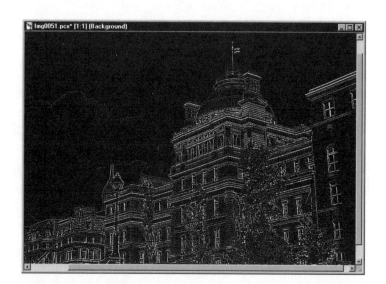

Using the Find Edges filter

If you only want to apply the filter to a part of the image, define the appropriate selection area first.

Use either of the following methods to launch the Find Edges filter:

The menu route

Pull down the Image menu and do the following:

Click here

2 Click here

The Browser route

Pull down the Image menu and click Filter Browser. Now do the following:

Click Find Edges

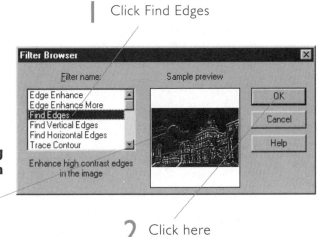

The effect of applying the chosen filter is previewed here:

2 Click here

The Horizontal Edges filter

The Find Horizontal Edges filter works by darkening an image and then emphasising its horizontal edges.

Use the Find Horizontal Edges filter when you need to identify – and emphasise – those parts of an image which have significant horizontal colour transitions.

The illustration below shows an image *before* the filter has been applied:

And now the result of applying the filter:

The Find Horizontal Edges filter produces results which are similar to the Find Edges filter, and just as dramatically creative.

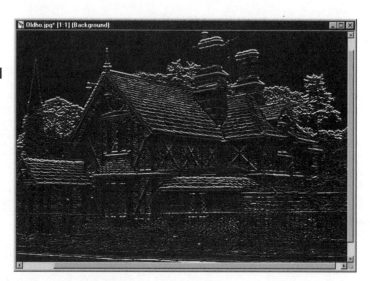

Using the Horizontal Edges filter

Use either of the following methods to launch the Find Horizontal Edges filter:

 If you only want to apply the filter to a part of the image, define the appropriate selection area first.

The menu route

Pull down the Image menu and do the following:

Click here

2 Click here

The Browser route

Pull down the Image menu and click Filter Browser. Now do the following:

Click Find Horizontal Edges

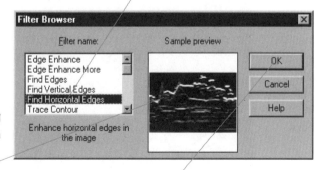

 The effect of applying the chosen filter is previewed here:

2 Click here

The Vertical Edges filter

Use the Find Vertical Edges filter when you need to identify – and emphasise – those parts of an image which have significant vertical colour transitions.

The illustration below shows an image *before* the filter has been applied:

The Find Vertical Edges filter works by darkening an image and then emphasising its vertical edges.

And now the result of applying the filter:

The Find Vertical Edges filter produces results which are similar to the Find Edges filter, and just as dramatically creative.

Using the Vertical Edges filter

If you only want to apply the filter to a part of the image, define the appropriate selection area first.

Use either of the following methods to launch the Find Vertical Edges filter:

The menu route

Pull down the Image menu and do the following:

Click here

2 Click here

The Browser route

Pull down the Image menu and click Filter Browser. Now do the following:

Click Find Vertical Edges

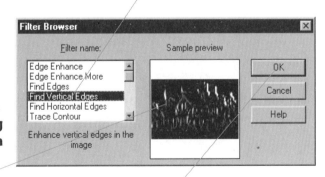

The effect of applying the chosen filter is previewed here:

2 Click here

The Trace Contour filter

The Trace Contour filter is a specialist edge filter which, effectively, outlines images by defining a border around them.

The illustration below shows an image *before* the Trace Contour filter has been applied:

The Trace Contour filter works by identifying areas of contrast, outlining them and whitening the remaining pixels.

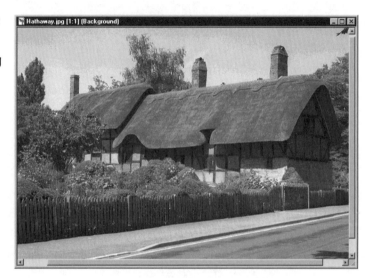

And now the result of applying the filter:

Using the Trace Contour filter

If you only want to apply the filter to a part of the image, define the appropriate selection area first.

Use either of the following methods to launch the Trace Contour filter:

The menu route

Pull down the Image menu and do the following:

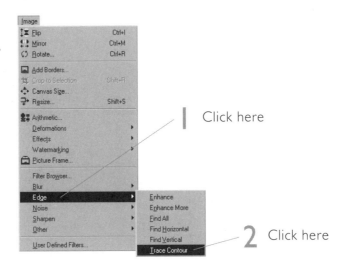

Click here

2 Click here

The Browser route

Pull down the Image menu and click Filter Browser. Now do the following:

Click Trace Contour

The effect of applying the chosen filter is previewed here:

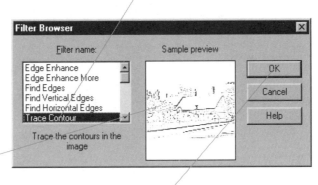

2 Click here

The Blur filter

You can use the Blur More filter to achieve an even more marked effect:

(See the DON'T FORGET tips on the facing page.)

Use these additional filters to achieve blur variations:

- **Motion Blur — adds direction to the blur, or;**
- **Gaussian Blur — blurs pixels incrementally**

To apply either of these, pull down the Image menu and select Blur. Now click Gaussian Blur or Motion Blur. Complete the dialog which launches, then click OK.

The Blur filter lightens pixels which adjoin the hard edges of defined lines and shaded areas, making for a hazy effect.

The illustration below shows an image *before* the Blur filter has been applied:

And now the result of applying the filter:

Using the Blur filter

If you only want to apply the filter to a part of the image, define the appropriate selection area first.

Use either of the following methods to launch the Blur filter:

The menu route

Pull down the Image menu and do the following:

Re step 2 – to apply the Blur More filter instead, select Blur More.

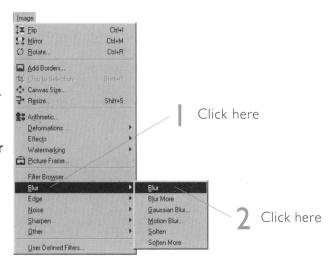

The Browser route

Pull down the Image menu and click Filter Browser. Now do the following:

Re step 1 – to apply the Blur More filter instead, select Blur More.

The effect of applying the chosen filter is previewed here:

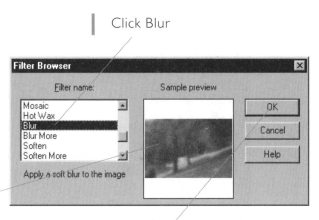

The Soften filter

The Soften filter diminishes image graininess.
By applying this filter more than once, you can simulate the effect of motion.

The Soften filter smooths out an image by decreasing the contrast between neighbouring pixels.

The illustration below shows an image *before* the Soften filter has been applied:

You can also use the Soften More filter to achieve an even more marked effect:

(See the DON'T FORGET tips on the facing page.)

And now the result of applying the filter:

Using the Soften filter

If you only want to apply the filter to a part of the image, define the appropriate selection area first.

Use either of the following methods to launch the Soften filter:

The menu route

Pull down the Image menu and do the following:

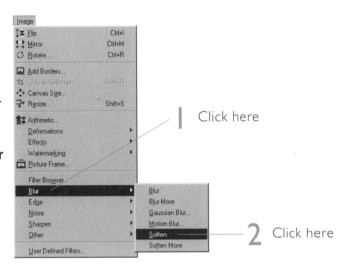

Click here

2 Click here

Re step 2 – to apply the Soften More filter instead, select Soften More.

The Browser route

Pull down the Image menu and click Filter Browser. Now do the following:

Re step 1 – to apply the Soften More filter instead, select Soften More.

The effect of applying the chosen filter is previewed here:

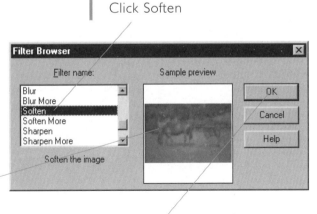

Click Soften

2 Click here

The Sharpen filter

You can also sharpen images (though in a different way) by using the paradoxically named Unsharpen filter.

Pull down the Image menu and click Sharpen, Unsharp Mask. In the Unsharp Mask dialog, adjust the settings in the Radius, Clipping and Strength fields appropriately.

Finally, click OK.

The Sharpen filter improves an image's focus and clarity.

The illustration below shows an image *before* the Sharpen filter has been applied:

And now the result of applying the filter:

You can also use the Sharpen More filter to achieve an even more marked effect:

(See the DON'T FORGET tips on the facing page.)

Using the Sharpen filter

 If you only want to apply the filter to a part of the image, define the appropriate selection area first.

Use either of the following methods to launch the Sharpen filter:

The menu route

Pull down the Image menu and do the following:

 Re step 2 – to apply the Sharpen More filter instead, select Sharpen More.

Click here

2 Click here

The Browser route

Pull down the Image menu and click Filter Browser. Now do the following:

 Re step 1 – to apply the Sharpen More filter instead, select Sharpen More.

Click Sharpen

 The effect of applying the chosen filter is previewed here:

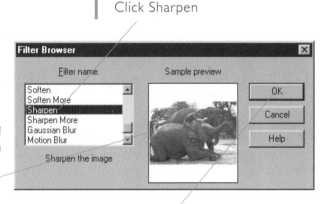

2 Click here

The Add Noise filter

The Add Noise filter ensures that images have randomly distributed colour pixels; you can determine, in a special dialog, the extent and type of the distribution.

The illustration below shows an image *before* the Add Noise filter has been applied:

Try adding small amounts of noise to images with imperfections: this can help to reduce defects.

Choose Uniform (see step 5 on the facing page) for an effect which (as here) more closely resembles the original image.

And now the result of applying the filter:

The Add Noise filter produces creative effects which would otherwise be very difficult and time-consuming to achieve.

Using the Add Noise filter

 If you only want to apply the filter to a part of the image, define the appropriate selection area first.

 Re step 4 – the permitted range is 1 (almost no noise) to 100 (maximum noise).

| Pull down the Image menu and do the following:

2 Click here

3 Click here

4 Specify the noise required

 You can also use the Filter Browser to apply noise.
   Pull down the Image menu and click Filter Browser. In the Filter name: field in the Browser, select Add Noise. Click OK. Now complete steps 4-6 on the right.

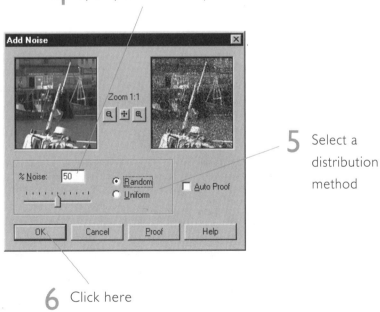

5 Select a distribution method

6 Click here

The Despeckle filter

The Despeckle filter blurs all of an image except those locations (edges) where meaningful colour changes take place.

The illustration below shows an image *before* the Despeckle filter has been applied:

You can sometimes use Despeckle to remove small scratches in images.

And now the result of applying the filter:

Notice how the Despeckle filter blurs the contents of the magnifying lens.

Using the Despeckle filter

 If you only want to apply the filter to a part of the image, define the appropriate selection area first.

Use either of the following methods to launch the Despeckle filter:

The menu route
Pull down the Image menu and do the following:

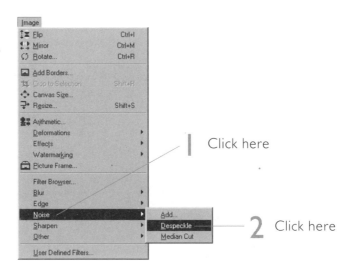

Click here

2 Click here

The Browser route
Pull down the Image menu and click Filter Browser. Now do the following:

Click Despeckle

 **The effect of applying the chosen filter is previewed here:**

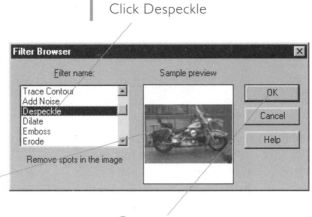

2 Click here

The Dilate filter

The Dilate filter enhances light areas in an image.

The illustration below shows an image *before* the Dilate filter has been applied:

And now the result of applying the filter:

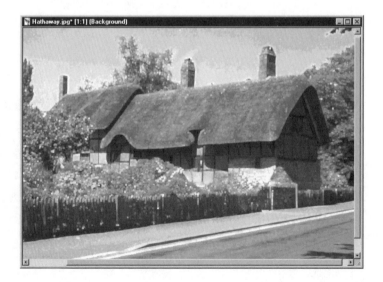

Using the Dilate filter

 If you only want to apply the filter to a part of the image, define the appropriate selection area first.

Use either of the following methods to launch the Dilate filter:

The menu route

Pull down the Image menu and do the following:

Click here

2 Click here

The Browser route

Pull down the Image menu and click Filter Browser. Now do the following:

Click Dilate

 **The effect of applying the chosen filter is previewed here:**

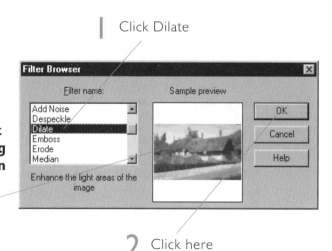

2 Click here

The Emboss filter

The Emboss filter gives images a raised effect.

The illustration below shows an image *before* the Emboss filter has been applied:

When the Emboss filter is applied, **areas of contrast are emphasised with black or white, while low-contrast areas are coloured grey.**

(If the contrast is marked enough, colours are retained.)

And now the result of applying the filter:

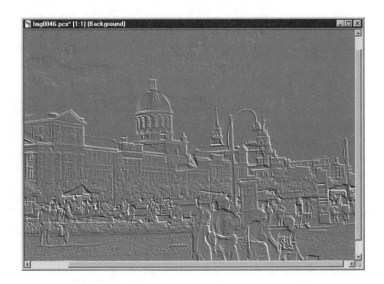

Using the Emboss filter

 If you only want to apply the filter to a part of the image, define the appropriate selection area first.

Use either of the following methods to launch the Emboss filter:

The menu route

Pull down the Image menu and do the following:

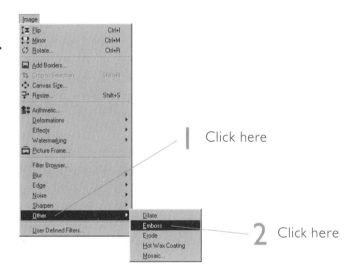

Click here

2 Click here

The Browser route

Pull down the Image menu and click Filter Browser. Now do the following:

Click Emboss

 **The effect of applying the chosen filter is previewed here:**

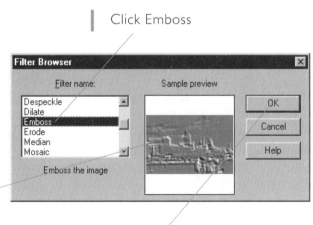

2 Click here

The Erode filter

The Erode filter emphasises dark areas in an image.

The illustration below shows an image *before* the Erode filter has been applied:

And now the result of applying the filter:

Using the Erode filter

If you only want to apply the filter to a part of the image, define the appropriate selection area first.

Use either of the following methods to launch the Erode filter:

The menu route

Pull down the Image menu and do the following:

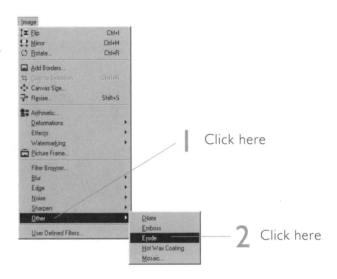

Click here

2 Click here

The Browser route

Pull down the Image menu and click Filter Browser. Now do the following:

Click Erode

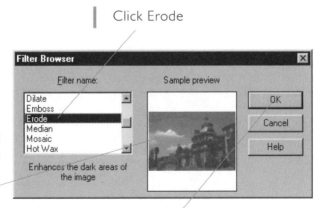

The effect of applying the chosen filter is previewed here:

2 Click here

The Median Cut filter

The Median Cut filter reduces image noise by 'averaging' pixel brightness and discarding pixels which have relatively little in common with their neighbours.

The illustration below shows an image *before* the Median Cut filter has been applied:

And now the result of applying the filter:

 **Notice how the Median Cut filter blurs the contents of the magnifying lens.**

Using the Median Cut filter

If you only want to apply the filter to a part of the image, define the appropriate selection area first.

Use either of the following methods to launch the Median Cut filter:

The menu route

Pull down the Image menu and do the following:

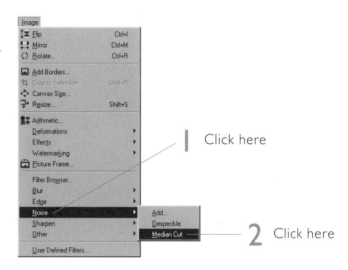

Click here

2 Click here

The Browser route

Pull down the Image menu and click Filter Browser. Now do the following:

Click Median

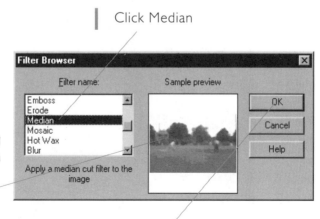

The effect of applying the chosen filter is previewed here:

2 Click here

The Mosaic filter

The Mosaic filter groups pixels into blocks, according to the block dimensions you specify.

The illustration below shows an image *before* the Mosaic filter has been applied:

And now the result of applying the filter:

 This effect was achieved with the following settings in the Mosaic dialog (see step 4 on the facing page): Block Width — 20 Block Height — 20

 Using higher settings produces a much more marked effect.

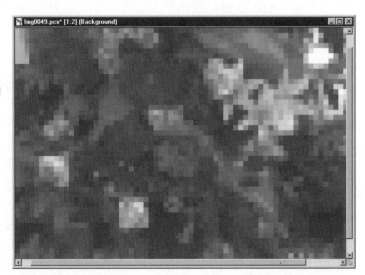

Using the Mosaic filter

 If you only want to apply the filter to a part of the image, define the appropriate selection area first.

 You can also use the Filter Browser to apply the Mosaic filter.

Pull down the Image menu and click Filter Browser. In the Filter name: field in the Browser, select Mosaic. Click OK. Now complete steps 4-5 on the right.

 Ensure Symmetric is activated to synchronise the Block Width and Block Height settings.

1 Pull down the Image menu and do the following:

2 Click here

3 Click here

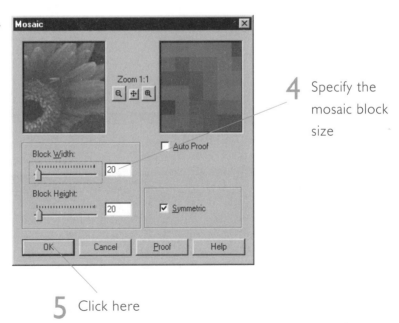

4 Specify the mosaic block size

5 Click here

The Hot Wax Coating filter

See chapter 7 for how to work with masks.

The Hot Wax Coating filter simulates dipping images (or selection areas/masks) in hot wax. Paint Shop Pro uses the current foreground colour in applying the wax effect.

The illustration below shows an image before the Hot Wax Coating filter has been applied:

And now the result of applying the filter:

Here, the Hot Wax Coating effect has been applied with the foreground colour as white.
   (See page 25 for how to specify foreground colours.)

Using the Hot Wax Coating filter

If you only want to apply the filter to a part of the image, define the appropriate selection area first.

Use either of the following methods to launch the Median filter:

The menu route

Pull down the Image menu and do the following:

Click here

2 Click here

The Browser route

Pull down the Image menu and click Filter Browser. Now do the following:

Click Hot Wax

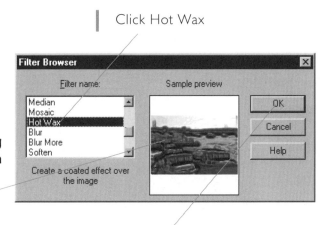

The effect of applying the chosen filter is previewed here:

2 Click here

User-defined filters

You can define your own filters, easily and conveniently. Once created, new filters can be named, saved and applied to images whenever required.

The next illustration shows an image *before* the application of a user-defined filter:

Applying this user-defined filter has arguably improved the image: the sky looks better.

Amending the Division factor (see step 4 on the facing page) can have a marked effect.
For instance, increasing it from 1 to 3 makes the image look like this:

And now the result of applying the filter:

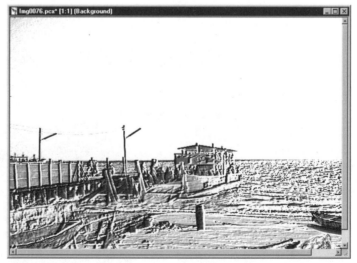

Creating filters

Defining your own filter

Pull down the Image menu and click User Defined Filters.
Now carry out the following steps:

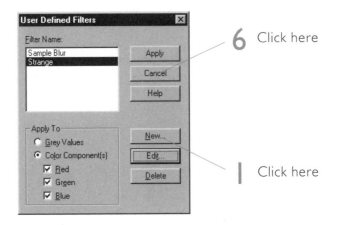

6 Click here

1 Click here

2 Name the new filter

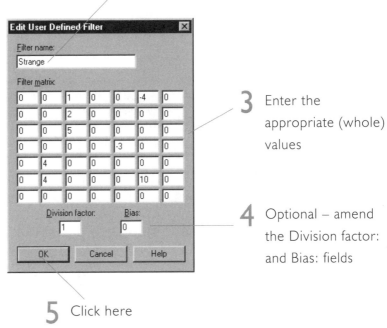

The settings shown here produce the effect demonstrated on the facing page.

3 Enter the appropriate (whole) values

4 Optional – amend the Division factor: and Bias: fields

5 Click here

Applying user-defined filters

1 Open the image you want to apply the filter to

2 Optional – to limit the effect of the filter, define the relevant selection area

3 Pull down the Image menu and carry out the following steps:

 To edit an existing user-defined filter, follow steps 1-5 on the right. Omit step 6. Instead, click this button:

In the Edit User Defined Filter dialog, make the relevant adjustments in line with steps 3-4 on page 123. Click OK. Click Cancel.
(Alternatively, follow step 6 on the right to apply the amended filter immediately.)

4 Click here

5 Select a filter

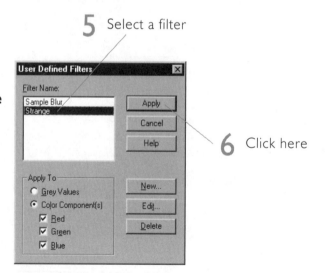

6 Click here

Using deformations

In this chapter, you'll add additional creative effects to images (or image selections) by applying specialist deformations.

Covers

Chapter Five

Deformations – an overview

In addition to the filters discussed in chapter 4, Paint Shop Pro also offers:

— a further series of filters (called deformations) which distort images

— a range of special effects – see chapter 6

The available deformations are:

- Circle
- Cylinder - Horizontal
- Cylinder - Vertical
- CurlyQs
- Pentagon
- Perspective - Horizontal
- Perspective - Vertical
- Pinch
- Punch
- Ripple
- Rotating Mirror
- Skew
- Spiky Halo
- Twirl
- Warp
- Wave
- Wind

Experiment with applying more than one deformation to images (or the same deformation more than once) – the results can be dramatic.

...cont'd

You can apply deformations in two ways:

- via a menu

- via the Deformation Browser

Both techniques are easy and convenient to use, but for some deformations (where there is no intermediary dialog which allows you to specify deformation settings), the Deformation Browser is especially useful.

 Images must fall into the following categories:

- **coloured images with more than 256 colours**
- **256-colour greyscales**

for deformations to work on them.

(If the image you want to apply a deformation to doesn't meet these criteria, carry out the procedure in the HOT TIP on page 89.)

The Deformation Browser

The Deformation Browser is a special dialog which lets you preview the effects of applying a deformation before you commit yourself to doing so.

It's also a way of accessing every available deformation, without having to pull down a succession of menus.

In the following illustration, the Deformation Browser is previewing the effect of applying the Skew deformation:

Deformations are previewed here

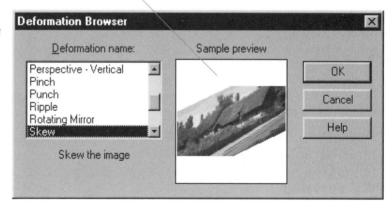

The Circle deformation

The Circle deformation produces a 'fish-eye' effect.

The illustration below shows an image after the Circle deformation has been applied:

 For how to use masks, see chapter 7.

Applying the Circle deformation

 To apply this deformation via a menu route, ignore steps 2-4. Instead, pull down the Image menu and select Deformations, Circle.

1 Optional – to limit the deformation to part of the image, define the relevant selection area or mask

2 Pull down the Image menu and select Deformations, Deformation Browser

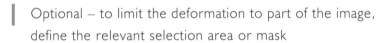 3 Click Circle

 The result of applying the chosen deformation is previewed here:

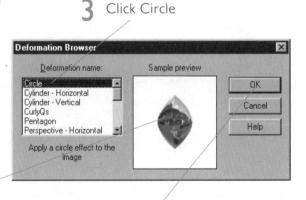

 4 Click here

The CurlyQs deformation

The CurlyQs deformation splits images into curled columns.

The illustration below shows an image after the CurlyQs deformation has been applied:

If you want to limit the deformation to a selection area or mask, define it before step 1.

Applying the CurlyQs deformation

1 Pull down the Image menu and select Deformations, Deformation Browser

2 In the Deformation name: field in the Browser, select CurlyQs then click OK

To apply this deformation via a menu route, ignore steps 1-2. Instead, pull down the Image menu and select Deformations, CurlyQs. Now complete steps 3-5.

3 Specify the no. of columns/rows

You can also specify the deformation direction. Choose Clockwise or CounterClockwise.

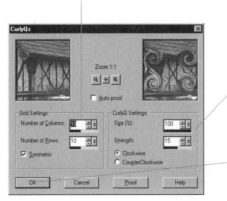

4 Specify the CurlyQ size and strength

5 Click here

The Cylinder deformations

Of the two cylinder deformations, the Cylinder - Horizontal deformation stretches an image horizontally, while the Cylinder - Vertical deformation stretches it vertically.

See the examples below:

The original image

After applying the Cylinder - Horizontal deformation

After applying the Cylinder - Vertical deformation

Using the Cylinder deformations

If you want to limit the deformation to a part of the image, define the appropriate selection area or mask first.

1 Pull down the Image menu and do the following:

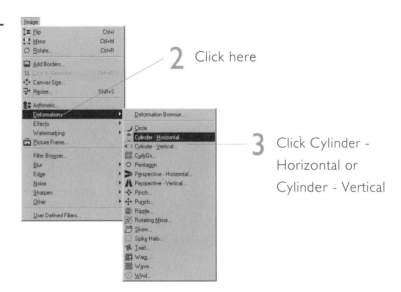

2 Click here

3 Click Cylinder - Horizontal or Cylinder - Vertical

**You can also use the Deformation Browser to apply this deformation.
Pull down the Image menu and click Deformations, Deformation Browser. In the Deformation name: field in the Browser, select Cylinder - Horizontal or Cylinder - Vertical. Click OK. Now complete steps 4-5 on the right.**

4 Drag the slider to the required setting

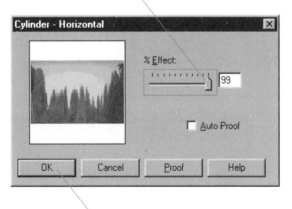

5 Click here

The Pentagon deformation

The Pentagon deformation transforms an image into a five-sided figure.

The illustration below shows an image after the Pentagon deformation has been applied:

To apply this deformation via a menu route, ignore steps 2-4. Instead, pull down the Image menu and select Deformations, Pentagon.

Applying the Pentagon deformation

1 Optional – to limit the deformation to part of the image, define the relevant selection area or mask

2 Pull down the Image menu and select Deformations, Deformation Browser

3 Click Pentagon

The result of applying the deformation is previewed here:

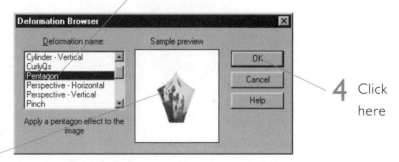

4 Click here

The Perspective deformations

There are two perspective deformations. The Perspective - Horizontal deformation slants an image horizontally, while the Perspective - Vertical deformations slants it vertically. The result incorporates a perspective effect:

The original image

After applying the Perspective - Horizontal deformation

After applying the Perspective - Vertical deformation

Using the Perspective deformations

If you want to limit the deformation to a part of the image, define the appropriate selection area or mask first.

Pull down the Image menu and do the following:

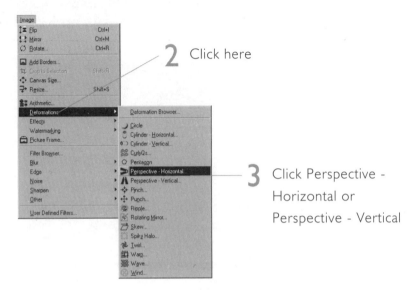

2 Click here

3 Click Perspective - Horizontal or Perspective - Vertical

You can also use the Deformation Browser to apply this deformation.
  Pull down the Image menu and click Deformations, Deformation Browser. In the Deformation name: field in the Browser, select Perspective - Horizontal or Perspective - Vertical. Click OK. Now complete steps 4-5 on the right.

4 Drag the slider to the required setting

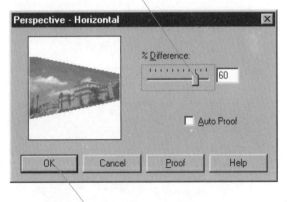

5 Click here

The Pinch deformation

Pinching is the opposite of the Punch deformation (see overleaf).

The Pinch deformation compresses an image towards its centre.

The illustration below shows an image after the Pinch deformation has been applied:

To apply this deformation via a menu route, ignore steps 2-3. Instead, pull down the Image menu and select Deformations, Pinch. Now complete steps 4-5.

Applying the Pinch deformation

1 Optional – to limit the deformation to part of the image, define the relevant selection area or mask

2 Pull down the Image menu and select Deformations, Deformation Browser

3 In the Deformation name: field in the Browser, select Pinch then click OK

4 Drag the slider to the required setting

The result of applying the deformation is previewed here:

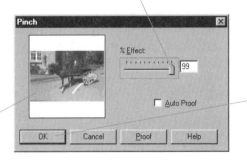

5 Click here

The Punch deformation

The Punch deformation expands images from the centre.

The illustration below shows an image after the Punch deformation has been applied:

To apply this deformation via a menu route, ignore steps 2-3. Instead, pull down the Image menu and select Deformations, Punch. Now complete steps 4-5.

Applying the Punch deformation

1 Optional – to limit the deformation to part of the image, define the relevant selection area or mask

2 Pull down the Image menu and select Deformations, Deformation Browser

3 In the Deformation name: field in the Browser, select Punch then click OK

4 Drag the slider to the required setting

The result of applying the deformation is previewed here:

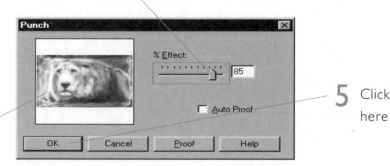

5 Click here

The Ripple deformation

If you want to limit the deformation to a selection area or mask, define it before step 1.

The Ripple deformation defines concentric rings around (by default) an image's midpoint.

The illustration below shows an image after the Ripple deformation has been applied:

To apply this deformation via a menu route, ignore steps 1-2. Instead, pull down the Image menu and select Deformations, Ripple. Now complete steps 3-5.

Applying the Ripple deformation

1 Pull down the Image menu and select Deformations, Deformation Browser

2 In the Deformation name: field in the Browser, select Ripple then click OK

Re step 3 – the amplitude is the distance from the peak of each ripple to its base; the wavelength is the distance between each peak.

3 Drag these sliders to specify the amplitude and wavelength

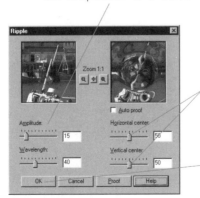

Re step 4 – these settings specify the ripple position relative to the image centre.

4 Drag these sliders to the required setting

5 Click here

The Rotating Mirror deformation

The Rotating Mirror deformation reflects part of an image on itself (you can vary the angle of rotation).

The illustration below shows an image after the Rotating Mirror deformation has been applied:

If you want to limit the deformation to a selection area or mask, define it before step 1.

To apply this deformation via a menu route, ignore steps 1-2. Instead, pull down the Image menu and select Deformations, Rotating Mirror. Now complete steps 3-4.

Applying the Rotating Mirror deformation

1 Pull down the Image menu and select Deformations, Deformation Browser

2 In the Deformation name: field in the Browser, select Rotating Mirror then click OK

Also complete the fields in the Mirror Placement section; these control the reflection's positioning relative to the image centre.

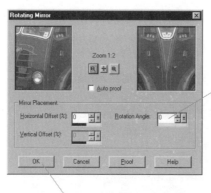

3 Specify a rotation angle

4 Click here

The Skew deformation

The Skew deformation slants images.

You can skew in two (mutually exclusive) directions:
- **vertically, or;**
- **horizontally**

The illustration below shows an image after the Skew deformation has been applied:

Horizontal Skew in action

Applying the Skew deformation

To apply this deformation via a menu route, ignore steps 2-3. Instead, pull down the Image menu and select Deformations, Skew. Now complete steps 4-5.

1 Optional – to limit the deformation to part of the image, define the relevant selection area or mask

2 Pull down the Image menu and select Deformations, Deformation Browser

3 In the Deformation name: field in the Browser, select Skew then click OK

4 Drag one of the sliders to the required setting

The result of applying the deformation is previewed here:

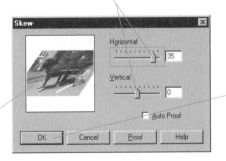

5 Click here

The Spiky Halo deformation

If you want to limit the deformation to a selection area or mask, define it before step 1.

The Spiky Halo deformation applies a crown of waves arranged radially.

The illustration below shows an image after the Spiky Halo deformation has been applied:

To apply this deformation via a menu route, ignore steps 1-2. Instead, pull down the Image menu and select Deformations, Spiky Halo. Now complete steps 3-4.

Applying the Spiky Halo deformation

1 Pull down the Image menu and select Deformations, Deformation Browser

2 In the Deformation name: field in the Browser, select Spiky Halo then click OK

Re step 3 – the amplitude is the distance from the peak of each wave to its base; the frequency is the number of rays.

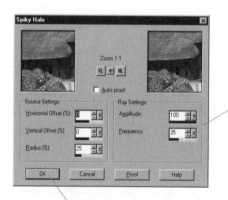

3 Specify the amplitude and frequency

Also complete the fields in the Source Settings section; these control the halo's positioning.

4 Click here

The Twirl deformation

The Twirl deformation rotates an image around its centre.

The illustration below shows an image after the Twirl deformation has been applied:

 If you want to limit the deformation to a selection area or mask, define it before step 1.

 To apply this deformation via a menu route, ignore steps 1-2. Instead, pull down the Image menu and select Deformations, Twirl. Now complete steps 3-4.

 Re step 3 – minus settings produce an anti-clockwise rotation.

Applying the Twirl deformation

1 Pull down the Image menu and select Deformations, Deformation Browser

2 In the Deformation name: field in the Browser, select Twirl then click OK

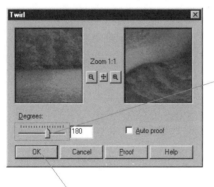

3 Drag the slider to specify the degree of Twirl

4 Click here

The Warp deformation

The Warp deformation magnifies an image's centre in relation to the remainder.

The illustration below shows an image after the Warp deformation has been applied:

If you want to limit the deformation to a selection area or mask, define it before step 1.

To apply this deformation via a menu route, ignore steps 1-2. Instead, pull down the Image menu and select Deformations, Warp. Now complete steps 3-4.

Applying the Warp deformation

1 Pull down the Image menu and select Deformations, Deformation Browser

2 In the Deformation name: field in the Browser, select Warp then click OK

Re step 3 – the strength is the degree of magnification; the size is self-explanatory.

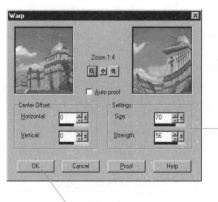

3 Specify the size and strength

Also complete the fields in the Center Offset: section; these control the position of the deformation centre.

4 Click here

The Wave deformation

The Wave deformation imposes undulating vertical and horizontal lines.

The illustration below shows an image after the Wave deformation has been applied:

If you want to limit the deformation to a selection area or mask, define it before step 1.

To apply this deformation via a menu route, ignore steps 1-2. Instead, pull down the Image menu and select Deformations, Wave. Now complete steps 3-4.

Re step 3 – the amplitude is the distance from the peak of each ripple to its base; the wavelength is the distance between each peak.

Applying the Wave deformation

1 Pull down the Image menu and select Deformations, Deformation Browser

2 In the Deformation name: field in the Browser, select Wave then click OK

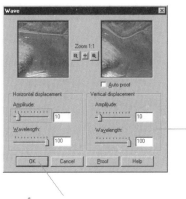

3 Specify the horizontal/ vertical amplitude and wavelength

4 Click here

The Wind deformation

You can apply wind in either of two directions:

- **from right to left, or;**
- **from left to right**

The Wind deformation inserts horizontal (very thin) lines into images, an effect which mimics wind.

The illustration below shows an image after the Wind deformation has been applied:

Wind from right to left

Applying the Wind deformation

To apply this deformation via a menu route, ignore steps 2-3. Instead, pull down the Image menu and select Deformations, Wind. Now complete steps 4-6.

1 Optional – to limit the deformation to part of the image, define the relevant selection area or mask

2 Pull down the Image menu and select Deformations, Deformation Browser

3 In the Deformation name: field in the Browser, select Wind then click OK

4 Drag the slider to the required setting

The result of applying the deformation is previewed here:

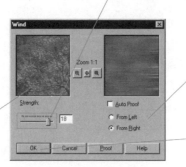

5 Select a direction

6 Click here

Using effects

In this chapter, you'll enhance images (or image selections) by applying any of Paint Shop Pro's numerous special effects.

Covers

Chapter Six

Effects – an overview

In addition to the filters discussed in chapter 4 and the deformations described in chapter 5, Paint Shop Pro also offers a range of special effects.

These additional effects are:

You can also apply any of a series of six related effects which make images look as if they have been drawn with special media:

- **Black Pencil**
- **Colored Chalk**
- **Colored Pencil**
- **Charcoal**
- **Glowing Edges, and;**
- **Neon Glow**

Experiment with applying more than one effect to images (or the same effect more than once) – the results can be dramatic.

- Blinds
- Buttonize
- Chisel
- Chrome
- Cutout
- Drop Shadow
- Feedback
- Inner Bevel
- Kaleidoscope
- Mosaic - Antique
- Mosaic - Glass
- Outer Bevel
- Pattern
- Sculpture
- Texture
- Tiles
- Weave

The Black Pencil effect

The Black Pencil effect mimics the result of drawing with a black pencil.

 Images must fall into the following categories:

The illustration below shows an image after the Black Pencil effect has been applied:

- coloured images with more than 256 colours, or;
- 256-colour greyscales

for effects to work on them.

(If the image you want to apply an effect to doesn't meet these criteria, carry out the procedure in the HOT TIP on page 89.)

Applying the Black Pencil effect

1 Optional – to restrict the effect, define a selection area

2 Pull down the Image menu and select Effects, Black Pencil

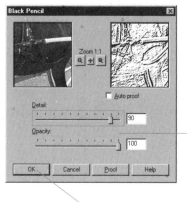

Re step 3 – the Detail slider sets the number of strokes used; the Opacity slider determines the effect's intensity.

3 Drag the Detail & Opacity sliders to the required settings

4 Click here

The Blinds effect

The Blinds effect mimics the result of applying horizontal or vertical blinds.

The illustration below shows an image after the Blinds effect has been applied:

 To specify a colour for the edges of the blinds, click the Color: field. In the Color dialog, select a new colour. Click OK.

 By default, blinds are lit from the bottom or right. To reverse this, select Light from left/top.

Applying the Blinds effect

1 Optional – to restrict the effect, define a selection area

2 Pull down the Image menu and select Effects, Blinds

 By default, blinds are horizontal. To make them vertical, deselect Horizontal.

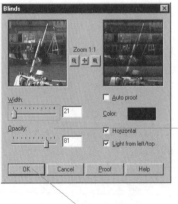

 Re step 3 – the Width slider sets the blind width; the Opacity slider determines the effect's intensity.

3 Drag the Width & Opacity sliders to the required settings

4 Click here

The Buttonize effect

The Buttonize effect applies a raised 3-D border.

The illustration below shows a bitmap rectangle after the Buttonize effect has been applied:

 See the DON'T FORGET tips on pages 156 and 159 for other ways to apply 3-D effects.

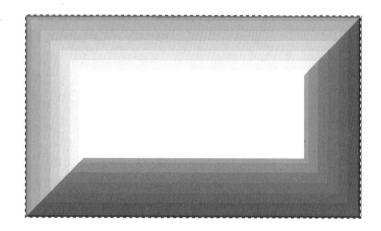

Applying the Buttonize effect

1 Optional – to limit the effect to part of an image, define the relevant selection area

2 Pull down the Image menu and select Effects, Buttonize

3 Drag the Height, Width & Opacity sliders to the required settings

 Select Solid Edge to have Paint Shop Pro use the current background colour to apply solid edges to the button.

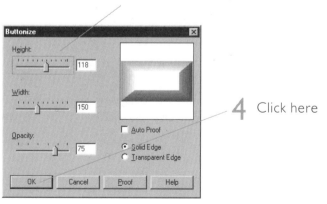

4 Click here

The Charcoal effect

The Charcoal effect resembles the Black Pencil effect; the difference is that it has more detail.

The Charcoal effect mimics the result of drawing with charcoal.

The illustration below shows an image after the Charcoal effect has been applied:

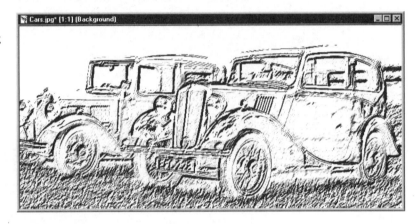

Applying the Charcoal effect

1 Optional – to restrict the effect, define a selection area

2 Pull down the Image menu and select Effects, Charcoal

Re step 3 – the Detail slider sets the number of strokes used; the Opacity slider determines the effect's intensity.

3 Drag the Detail & Opacity sliders to the required settings

4 Click here

The Chrome effect

The Chrome effect applies a metallic patina.

The illustration below shows an image after the Chrome effect has been applied:

Applying the Chrome effect

1 Optional – to restrict the effect, define a selection area

2 Pull down the Image menu and select Effects, Chrome

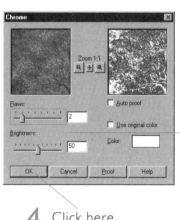

3 Drag the Flaws & Brightness sliders to the required settings

4 Click here

The Colored Chalk effect

The Colored Chalk effect mimics the result of drawing with coloured chalk.

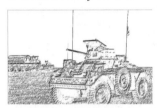

You can also make an image look as if it has been drawn with a coloured pencil:

The illustration below shows an image after the Colored Chalk effect has been applied:

Follow step 1, if applicable. In step 2, click Colored Pencil in the Image menu. Now carry out steps 3-4.

Applying the Colored Chalk effect

1 Optional – to restrict the effect, define a selection area

2 Pull down the Image menu and select Effects, Colored Chalk

Re step 3 – the Detail slider sets the number of strokes used; the Opacity slider determines the effect's intensity.

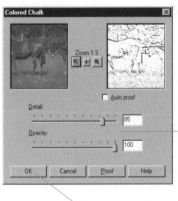

3 Drag the Detail & Opacity sliders to the required settings

4 Click here

The Cutout effect

You can convert a selection area into a 'cutout'. You then have the impression of looking through the image to a recessed area.

The illustration below shows an image after the Cutout effect has been applied:

Re step 3 – if Fill interior with color is selected, click in the Interior color: field. In the Color dialog, select a fill colour then click OK.

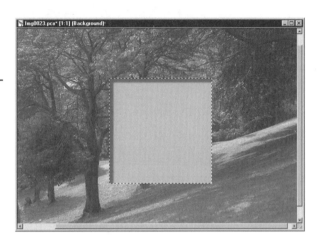

Applying the Cutout effect

Re step 4 – the Opacity slider determines the effect's intensity; the Blur slider widens and softens the cutout shadow.

1 Define the relevant selection area

2 Pull down the Image menu and select Effects, Cutout

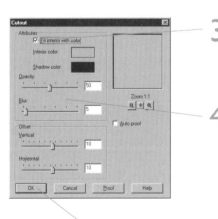

Also complete the fields in the Offset: section; these control the position of the cutout's interior.

3 Select Fill interior with color if you don't want the cutout filled with the image

4 Drag the Opacity & Blur sliders to the required settings

5 Click here

The Drop Shadow effect

The Drop Shadow effect only works with selection areas.

The Drop Shadow effect imposes a shadow behind selection areas.

The illustration below shows an image after the Drop Shadow effect has been applied:

To apply a drop shadow to the whole of an image (as here), carry out the following extra procedures before step 1:

- **press Ctrl+A (to select the entire image), and;**
- **follow the procedures on page 15 to increase the image's canvas (so the shadow can display)**

Applying the Drop Shadow effect

1 Define the relevant selection area

2 Pull down the Image menu and select Effects, Drop Shadow

3 Drag the Opacity & Blur sliders to the required settings

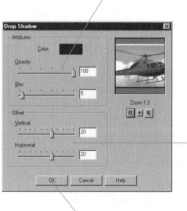

4 Drag the Vertical & Horizontal sliders to the required settings (to specify the shadow's position)

Re step 3 – the Opacity slider sets the drop shadow density; the ßlur slider determines its softness.

5 Click here

The Feedback effect

The Feedback effect makes an image appear to be reflected inwards in a series of concentric mirrors.

The illustration below shows an image after the Feedback effect has been applied:

 Re step 3 – the Opacity slider determines the effect's intensity; the Intensity slider sets the mirror frequency.

 Also complete the Horizontal center: and Vertical center: fields; these control the position of the feedback centre.

Applying the Feedback effect

1 Optional – to restrict the effect, define a selection area

2 Pull down the Image menu and select Effects, Feedback

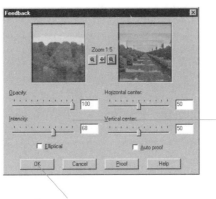

3 Drag the Opacity & Intensity sliders to the required settings

4 Click here

The Glowing Edges effect

The Glowing Edges effect colours image edges in neon (other image parts are blackened).

 To apply a 3-D effect to the interior of a selection area, first define the area. Pull down the Image menu and choose Effects, Inner Bevel. Click in the Presets: field in the Inner Bevel dialog; in the list, select a preset bevel effect.
Finally, click OK.

The illustration below shows an image after the Glowing Edges effect has been applied:

Applying the Glowing Edges effect

1 Optional – to restrict the effect, define a selection area

2 Pull down the Image menu and select Effects, Glowing Edges

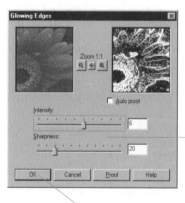 **Re step 3 – the Intensity slider controls edge brightness; the Sharpness slider is self-explanatory.**

3 Drag the Intensity & Sharpness sliders to the required settings

4 Click here

The Kaleidoscope effect

 When you apply the Kaleidoscope effect, Paint Shop Pro defines a (loosely) pie-shaped area at the centre of the image; this is surrounded by a circular pattern.
(The setting specified by step 3 controls the width of the outer edge.)

The Kaleidoscope effect mimics looking at an image through a kaleidoscope.

The illustration below shows an image after the Kaleidoscope effect has been applied:

 Also complete the fields in the Image Sector section; these control which portion of the image is used to create the outer circle.

Applying the Kaleidoscope effect

1   Optional – to restrict the effect, define a selection area

2   Pull down the Image menu and select Effects, Kaleidoscope

 Entering a value in the Radial Suction: field specifies the place in the inner pie from which Paint Shop Pro derives its pattern data.

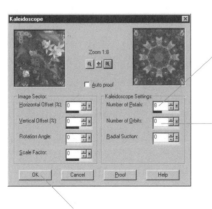

3   Specify the number of petals

4   Optional – specify the number of pattern repeats

5   Click here

The Mosaic - Antique effect

You can also tile images with glass:

Follow step 1, as applicable. In step 2, select Effects, Mosaic - Glass. Now carry out steps 3-4.

The Mosaic - Antique effect mimics applying antique tiles to an image.

The illustration below shows an image after the Mosaic - Antique effect has been applied:

Applying the Mosaic - Antique effect

1 Optional – to restrict the effect, define a selection area

2 Pull down the Image menu and select Effects, Mosaic - Antique

Optionally, also complete the fields in the Grid Settings section:

- **Tile Opacity —** specifies how much of the underlying image shows through
- **Grout Width —** specifies the gap between tiles, and;
- **Grout Opacity —** specifies the opacity of the gap between tiles

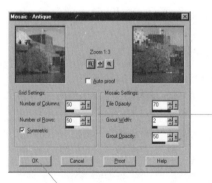

3 Specify the number of columns and rows

4 Click here

The Neon Glow effect

To apply a 3-D effect to part of an image, define the relevant selection area. Pull down the Image menu and choose Effects, Outer Bevel. Click in the Presets: field in the Outer Bevel dialog; in the list, select a preset bevel effect. Finally, click OK.

The Neon Glow effect mimics applying neon colours to an image.

The illustration below shows an image after the Neon Glow effect has been applied:

Applying the Neon Glow effect

1 Optional – to restrict the effect, define a selection area

2 Pull down the Image menu and select Effects, Neon Glow

Re step 3 – the Detail slider sets the number (and brightness) of colours used; the Opacity slider determines the effect's intensity.

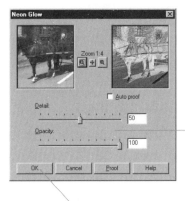

3 Drag the Detail & Opacity sliders to the required settings

4 Click here

The Pattern effect

The Pattern effect creates patterns from any image.

The illustration below shows an image after the Pattern effect has been applied:

 You can use patterns created by this effect in Web page backgrounds.

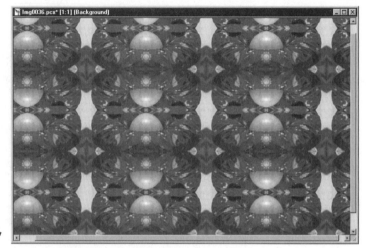

 Optionally, also complete the fields in the Image Area: section:

- **The Offset fields — specify where the pattern begins (the default is the image centre)**
- **Rotation Angle — to rotate the effect, enter the relevant angle, and;**
- **Scale Factor — specifies pattern size (the smaller the pattern, the more it repeats)**

Applying the Pattern effect

1 Optional – to restrict the effect, define a selection area

2 Pull down the Image menu and select Effects, Pattern

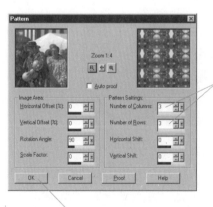

3 Specify the number of rows/columns

4 Click here

The Sculpture effect

Re step 3 – presets are ready-made formatting collections which give professional results. However, you can also omit step 3 and apply your own effect settings instead. For example:

- **to apply a new background pattern, click in the Pattern box; in the list, select a new one**
- **to apply a coloured light, click in the Color box; in the list, select a colour and click OK**
- **to customise the sculpture itself, amend the fields in the Image section**
- **to adjust the light origin, type in a new angle in the Angle: field**

Finally, when you've finished entering your own settings follow step 4.

The Sculpture effect combines embossing with the application of a coloured pattern.

The illustration below shows a bitmap rectangle after the Sculpture effect has been applied:

The 'Gold' preset

Applying the Sculpture effect

1 Optional – to limit the effect to part of an image, define the relevant selection area

2 Pull down the Image menu and select Effects, Sculpture

3 Click here; in the list, select a preset

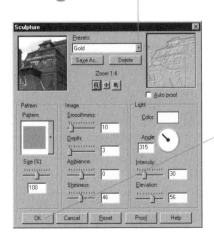

4 Click here

The Texture effect

Re step 3 – presets are ready-made formatting collections which give professional results. However, you can also omit step 3 and apply your own effect settings instead. For example:

- **to apply a new background pattern, click in the Pattern box; in the list, select a new one**
- **to apply a coloured light, click in the Color box; in the list, select a colour and click OK**
- **to customise the sculpture itself, amend the fields in the Image section**
- **to adjust the light origin, type in a new angle in the Angle: field**

Finally, when you've finished entering your own settings follow step 4.

The Texture effect mimics the result of painting an image onto a textured medium.

The illustration below shows an image after the Texture effect has been applied:

The 'Wrinkled' preset

Applying the Texture effect

1 Optional – to limit the effect to part of an image, define the relevant selection area

2 Pull down the Image menu and select Effects, Texture

3 Click here; in the list, select a preset

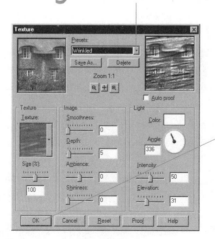

4 Click here

The Tiles effect

Re step 3 – presets are ready- made formatting collections which give professional results. However, you can also omit step 3 and apply your own effect settings instead. For example:

- **to apply a new background pattern, click in the Pattern box; in the list, select a new one**
- **to apply a coloured light, click in the Color box; in the list, select a colour and click OK**
- **to customise the sculpture itself, amend the fields in the Image section**
- **to adjust the light origin, type in a new angle in the Angle: field**

Finally, when you've finished entering your own settings follow step 4.

The Tiles effect makes an image look as though it was created from tiles.

The illustration below shows a bitmap rectangle after the Tiles effect has been applied:

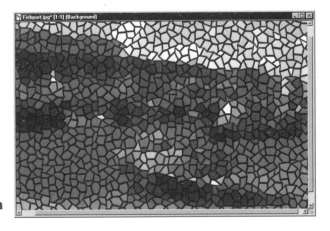

The 'Stained Glass' preset

Applying the Tiles effect

1 Optional – to limit the effect to part of an image, define the relevant selection area

2 Pull down the Image menu and select Effects, Tiles

3 Click here; in the list, select a preset

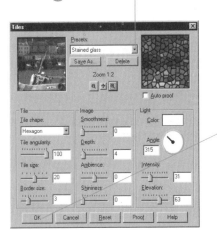

4 Click here

The Weave effect

The Weave effect applies a basketwork effect to images.

The illustration below shows an image after the Weave effect has been applied:

If you want the gap between strands to be filled with the image (rather than a colour), deselect Fill gaps.

By default, the weave colour is black. To apply a new one, click the Weave color: field. In the Color dialog, select it, then click OK.

Applying the Weave effect

1 Optional – to restrict the effect, define a selection area

2 Pull down the Image menu and select Effects, Weave

To specify the gap between strands, drag the Gap size: slider to the correct setting.

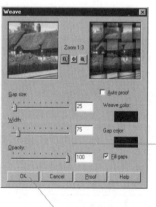

Re step 3 – the Width slider sets the thickness of each individual strand; the Opacity slider determines the effect's intensity.

3 Drag the Width & Opacity sliders to the required settings

4 Click here

Advanced techniques

In this chapter, you'll learn how to apply borders/frames to images; carry out screen captures; work with layers; and apply/edit masks. Then you'll crop images; work with histograms to readjust colour values; and carry out other colour corrections (including Posterize/Solarize). Finally, you'll convert images in batches, then preview – and print – your work (including multiple image printing).

Covers

Chapter Seven

Advanced techniques – an overview

Paint Shop Pro lets you carry out a wide assortment of advanced operations. You can:

- border or frame images very easily and conveniently

- capture Windows screens or screen components (and save them to disk as graphics files), including when Paint Shop Pro isn't running

- create and work with up to 100 image layers

- create masks (advanced selections which, in some ways, resemble stencils), and save them to disk for later use

- crop images (cropping is the removal of those sections of an image which are not required)

- carry out colour corrections. This involves:

    — viewing histograms (graphs displaying colour and luminance distribution)

    — using the histogram functions Equalize and Stretch

- convert colour images to greyscale

- invert ('negative') images

- customise other colour functions e.g. brightness/contrast and highlight/shadow

- Posterize and Solarize images

- converting groups of images into a new format, all in one operation

- preview images before printing

- print images (including arranging and printing images on a single sheet, from within a specialist window)

Bordering images

You can have Paint Shop Pro surround images with a border; this is defined with the current background colour. You can have each edge bordered automatically, or you can specify which edges should be affected.

If you want each border to be the same, omit step 4. Instead, ensure Symmetric is selected. Now complete any one of the edge fields. Finally, follow step 5.

Applying a border

1 Open the image you want to border

2 Use the techniques discussed on page 25 to select the relevant background colour

3 Pull down the Image menu and click Add Borders

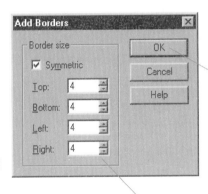

5 Click here

To add a frame to an image, pull down the Image menu and click Picture Frame. Click in the field in the Picture Frame Wizard dialog; in the list, select a frame effect. Finally, click Finish.

4 Type in the relevant border measurements

An image with a black border:

A framed image

Screen captures

You can have Paint Shop Pro create a snapshot of all or part of any Windows screen.

You can:

- specify which part of the screen is captured

- specify the signal which initiates the capture. You can use:

  — a keystroke combination (known as a 'hotkey') – e.g. F11 or Alt+F1

  — the right mouse button

- include the cursor in the capture

Having Paint Shop Pro perform a screen capture consists of the following sequential stages:

A. arrange the screen appropriately (this includes making the program whose screen you want to capture active)

B. switch to Paint Shop Pro

C. tell Paint Shop Pro to initiate a capture (at which point it minimises)

D. issue the capture signal

E. return to Paint Shop Pro (the captured screen automatically occupies its own window) and perform any necessary editing actions (e.g. cropping or converting to greyscale)

F. using standard procedures to save the screen capture as a graphics file for later use

HOT TIP

In programs (like Word 2000) which support OLE (Object Linking and Embedding), you can capture screens without running Paint Shop Pro.
In the OLE-compliant program, activate the 'Insert Object' command (usually Insert Object in the Insert menu). In the Object dialog, activate the Create New tab and double-click Paint Shop Pro 6 Screen Capture. Follow steps 1-3 on the facing page, then click OK. Go to the screen you want to capture and follow step D. on the right.
The captured screen is inserted into the OLE-compliant program.

...cont'd

Performing a screen capture

Perform steps A and B on the facing page. Now pull down the Capture menu and click Setup. Do the following:

Re step 3 – do this if you want to capture the cursor e.g.:

Paint Shop Pro's Zoom cursor

(You can't capture the cursor if you selected Area in step 1.)

1 Select a region   2 Optional – select a trigger

3 Optional – ensure this is selected (see the tip)

4 Click here

Paint Shop Pro minimises, and you're returned to the application whose screen you want to capture. Now perform ONE of the following:

5 If you selected Area, Object, Window or Client area in step 1, place the cursor over the screen component you want to capture

6 If you selected Full Screen in step 1, place the cursor anywhere on the screen

Follow step D on the facing page. Additionally, if you selected Area in step 1 above:

7 Position the cursor at one corner of the area you want to capture. Left-click once, then place the cursor at the opposing corner and left-click again

Back in Paint Shop Pro, perform steps E and F on the facing page, as appropriate.

Using layers

Paint Shop Pro images are divided into 'layers'. Layers are separate, transparent levels which add a new dimension to image editing. Memory permitting, you can have as many as 100 layers.

You can paint (or apply effects to) specific layers. When you do this, unaffected areas in underlying layers remain visible until such time as you merge the layers.

There are three kinds of layer:

- Raster (hosts pixel-related data)

- Vector (holds vector objects e.g. shapes and text)

- Adjustment (contains colour correction data)

You can:

- add/delete layers

- reorder layers

- blend layers

After step 3 or 4, the Layer Properties dialog launches. Complete this. For example:

Adding new layers

| Refer to the Layer palette:

Toolbar

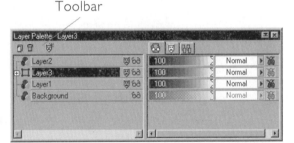

- **to name the layer, type in a name in the Name field in the General tab**
- **to specify the layer opacity, amend the value in the Opacity field in the General tab, or;**
- **(in adjustment layers) make the relevant amendments to the values in the Adjustment tab Finally, click OK.**

2 Right-click this button: in the Layer palette's toolbar

3 In the menu, choose New Raster Layer, New Vector Layer or New Adjustment Layer

4 If you chose New Adjustment Layer in step 3, also select a layer type (e.g. Hue/Saturation or Posterize)

...cont'd

 If the Layer palette isn't on-screen, right-click the Toolbar and select Layer Palette.

 To delete a layer, right-click it in the Layer palette. In the menu which launches, click Delete.

 By default, each image has a Background layer.

To promote this into a normal one, right-click it in the palette. In the menu, select Promote To Layer.

 To retain all layer information, follow the procedures in the HOT TIP on page 16 when saving your layered images.

Rearranging layers

1 Refer to the Layer palette:

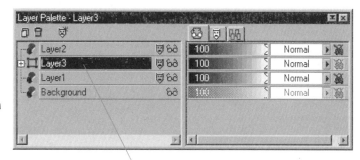

2 Click a layer, then drag it up or down to a new location in the palette

3 Release the mouse button

Merging layers

When you merge layers, you join all the component layers (or simply all visible layers) into one. As a result:

•   they can no longer be edited independently

•   all vector objects are rasterised

•   all transparent areas are whitened

1 Do ONE of the following, as appropriate:

2 To merge all the layers within an image, pull down the Layers menu and select Merge All (Flatten)

3 To merge only those layers currently visible within an image, pull down the Layers menu and select Merge Visible

Masks – an overview

The fact that masks are bitmaps means that all bitmap tools work with them.

Another corollary is that in those tools which have bitmap and vector modes (e.g. the Preset Shapes tool), only the bitmap component is operative on masks.

Masks are 256-colour greyscale bitmaps which are overlaid over image layers. They contain 'holes'; you perform editing operations on the areas displayed through the gaps. The holes can be created via:

- selection areas

- other images

Alternatively, the mask can be as large as the underlying layer.

To an extent, as we've seen, masks can be regarded as stencils. However, also implicit in the above description is the fact that they act as advanced selection areas. For example, you can control the extent to which a mask operates by defining the greyscale content:

— painting with black augments masking

— painting with white effaces masking

— any intervening shade of grey allows a portion of the effect you generate to take effect

You can apply any filter, deformation or effect which can be used with greyscale images.

Here, a separate image has been applied as a mask, and a fill applied

Layer masks

 You shouldn't apply masks to Background layers – instead, promote them first.
   (See the HOT TIP on page 171.)

You can create three principal types of mask:

- masks which apply to one specific layer

- selection masks (formed from, and based on, a pre-defined selection)

- image masks (based on a second image)

Masking an entire layer

 If the Layer palette isn't on-screen, right-click the Toolbar and select Layer Palette.

| Refer to the Layer palette:

Toolbar

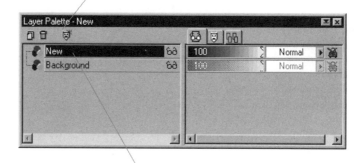

2 Select a layer

3 Do ONE of the following:

 Re step 4 – you can edit the mask later to unmask selective areas.

4 Left-click this button: in the Layer palette's toolbar – the entire layer is now masked

 Re step 5 – you can edit the mask later to mask selective areas.

5 Hold down Shift as you left-click this button: in the Layer palette's toolbar – as a result, the entire layer is now unmasked

Selection masks

To view a mask, press Ctrl+Alt+V.
(To hide it again, repeat this.)

Selection masks are masks which contain a hole (the hole being supplied by the selection area). By default, any changes you make apply to the hole, not the surrounding area.

Creating a selection mask

Define the appropriate selection area (see chapter 2 for how to do this). Now do the following:

Viewed masks are coloured red:

1 Refer to the Layer palette:

Toolbar

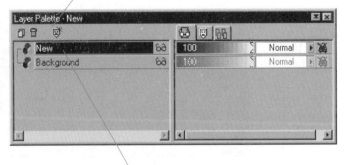

2 Select a layer

3 Do ONE of the following:

4 Right-click this button: in the Layer palette's toolbar, then do ONE of the following:

5 In the menu, click Hide Selection (to mask the selection)

After step 6, press Ctrl+D to remove the original selection area.

6 In the menu, click Show Selection (to mask everything apart from the selection)

Image masks

Creating masks from other images is a very useful technique. It can produce quite remarkable effects.

Creating masks from images

1 Open the image you want to use as a mask

2 Open the image into which you want to insert the mask

3 In the destination image, follow step 2 on the facing page

4 Pull down the Masks menu and click New, From Image

5 Click here; in the list, select the mask image

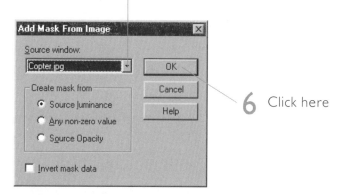

6 Click here

The result:

One image (COPTER.JPG) has been inserted over another as a mask

Editing masks

In particular, you can use the Fill tool to apply a new fill.

(See page 172 for a description of how colours influence the efficiency of masks.)

Paint Shop Pro has a special mode in which you can edit masks. This can involve:

- varying the extent of the mask (i.e. by painting over the object)

- painting the mask to control the degree (if any) of masking

Amending a mask

1 To view the mask, pull down the Masks menu and select View Mask

2 To enter Edit mode, press Ctrl+K

Re step 3 – use the following as guidelines:

- **paint with black to add masking**
- **paint with white to remove the mask, or;**
- **paint with grey shades to apply differing mask levels**

3 Alter the mask with any of the painting tools

4 To leave Edit mode, press Ctrl+K again

Reusing masks

Paint Shop Pro lets you save a mask to disk, as a special file (with the suffix .MSK). You can then load it into a new image. This is a convenient way to reuse masks.

Saving a mask

Define a mask. Pull down the Masks menu and click Save To Disk. Now do the following:

1 Click here. In the drop-down list, click a drive

Re step 2 – you may have to double-click one or more folders first, to locate the folder you want to save the mask to.

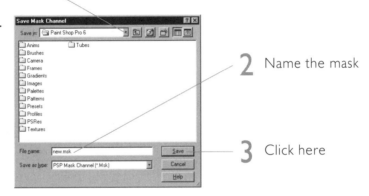

2 Name the mask

3 Click here

Loading a mask

Pull down the Masks menu and click Load From Disk. Now do the following:

1 Click here. In the drop-down list, click a drive

Re step 2 – you may have to double-click one or more folders first, to locate the folder which hosts the mask you want to open.

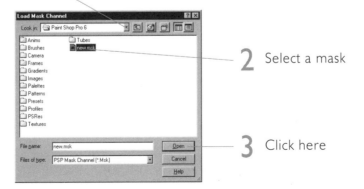

2 Select a mask

3 Click here

Cropping images

You crop images by:

1. defining the area you want to keep

2. telling Paint Shop Pro to discard the rest of the image

You can do this in two ways:

Cropping with selection areas

Define the relevant selection area, then pull down the Image menu and click Crop to Selection

An image
complete with
selection area

You can use the Crop tool to adjust the crop area you've just defined.

- **to move (but not resize) the crop rectangle, click inside it and drag to a new location, or;**
- **to resize the rectangle, move the cursor over one of the sides or corners, then drag in or out**

The result
of the crop

Cropping with the Crop tool

1 Click this tool: in the Toolbar

2 Place the mouse pointer at one corner of the area you want to retain

3 Hold down the left mouse button and drag over the area

4 Double-click inside the rectangle

Colour corrections – an overview

Paint Shop Pro lets you make various adjustments to image colour distribution. To help you decide which amendments are necessary, you can call up a special window: the Histogram viewer. Look at the illustrations below:

The original image

To open the Histogram viewer, simply press H. (To close it, press H again.)

Spike

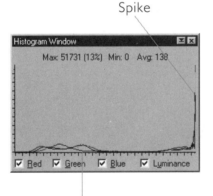

And its histogram

To convert a colour image to greyscale, pull down the Colors menu and click Grey Scale.

RGB and Luminance components

The Histogram window displays, along the horizontal axis, the three RGB components (Red, Green and Blue) together with Luminance. The vertical axis against which these are plotted represents each component's share of colours.

The far left of the horizontal axis represents black, the far right white. The 'spike' at the right of the histogram occurs because of the predominance of the sky in the illustration.

Histogram functions

To invert an image (convert its colours to their opposites), pull down the Colors menu and click Negative Image.

The image on the right, inverted

You can carry out two histogram-based operations on images: Equalize and Stretch.

Equalize rearranges image pixels so that those around the midpoint of the relevant histogram are pushed nearer the high and low brightness levels (see page 179 for more information). The result is normally an averaging of image brightness.

Stretch has somewhat the opposite effect. In images where black and white are not included in the histogram, it ensures the colours do span the full spectrum.

Applying Equalize or Stretch

If appropriate, define a selection area. Pull down the Colors menu and click Histogram Functions, Equalize OR Histogram Functions, Stretch.

To carry out a variety of further colour adjustments (e.g. amend brightness/contrast and highlight/shadow), pull down the Colors menu and click Adjust, followed by the relevant sub-option. Complete the dialog which launches, and click OK.

An unchanged image

And after applying Equalize

Solarize

Solarize inverts (reverses) colours which are over a user-set luminance threshold.

Paint Shop Pro has two further functions which manipulate image colours: Solarize and Posterize.

The illustration below shows the effect of applying the Solarize effect to the image on the facing page:

Re. step 3 – the permitted range is:

- **1 — maximum effect**
- **254 — minimum effect**

Re the above tip – setting the threshold at 1 is the same as inversion (see the HOT TIP on the facing page).

Solarizing an image

1 Optional – to restrict the effect, define a selection area

2 Pull down the Colors menu and select Solarize

3 Drag the Threshold slider to the required setting

4 Click here

Posterize

Posterize lets you specify an image's brightness value; the result amounts to a special effect.

The illustration below shows an image after the Posterize effect has been applied to the unchanged image on page 180:

Posterizing an image

1 Optional – to restrict the effect, define a selection area

2 Pull down the Colors menu and select Posterize

Re. step3 – the permitted range is:

- **2 — maximum effect**
- **255 — minimum effect**

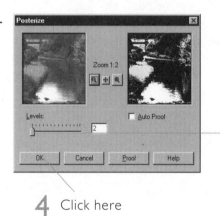

3 Drag the Levels slider to the required setting

4 Click here

Batch conversion – an overview

Chapter one explored:

- opening images

- saving them in alternative image formats

(see pages 10-11 and 16-17).

In effect, this amounts to converting images from one format to another, a process which is often indispensable when you work with pictures in Paint Shop Pro. For example, it's often very useful to convert images to TIFF (Tagged Image File Format) if you need to incorporate them into page layout programs...

However, converting images singly is at best a time-consuming process. It's also an unduly laborious one, because it consists (necessarily) of the two stages shown above. Fortunately, Paint Shop Pro lets you convert *multiple* image files, in one automated operation. It calls this Batch conversion.

Batch conversion consists of the following stages:

1. launching the Batch Conversion dialog

2. selecting an input folder (i.e. specifying the drive/folder combination which contains the images you want to convert)

3. selecting the files to be converted

4. selecting an output format (i.e. specifying the format you want the specified files converted to)

5. optional – specifying any additional output format options (e.g. selecting a compression type)

6. specifying an output folder (i.e. the drive/folder combination where you want the converted images stored)

Using batch conversion

Re step 3 – you may have to double-click one or more folders first, to locate the relevant images.

You can specify various output options – usually the compression type or colour depth of output files.

Click the Options button (if not greyed out), then complete the Save Options dialog. Click OK.

Finally, carry out step 6.

After step 6, a status dialog launches:

When conversion is complete, click OK.

Converting multiple images

Pull down the File menu and do the following:

1 Click here

2 Click here; select the input drive

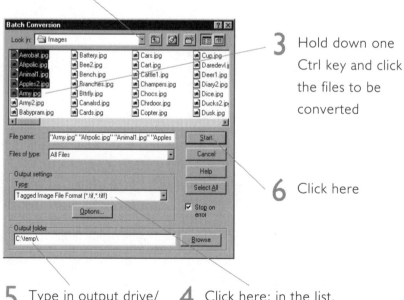

3 Hold down one Ctrl key and click the files to be converted

6 Click here

5 Type in output drive/ folder details

4 Click here; in the list, select an output format

Using Print Preview

To specify page setup settings, click this button in the toolbar:

`Setup...`

Make the relevant amendments in the Page Setup dialog. For example:

- **to print in greyscale (not colour), select Greyscale**
- **to centre the image on the page, select Center on page**
- **to print lengthways (not vertically), select Landscape**
- **to select a page size, click in the Size field; in the list, select a size, and/or;**
- **to use another printer, click the Printer button, select it in the new dialog then click OK**

Finally, click OK.

Paint Shop Pro provides a special view mode called Print Preview. This displays the active image exactly as it will look when printed. Use Print Preview as a final check just before you print your image.

You can customise the way Print Preview displays your image by zooming in or out on the active page. You can also specify page setup settings.

Launching Print Preview

Pull down the File menu and click Print Preview. This is the result:

Print Preview toolbar

Zooming in and out in Print Preview

To zoom in (increase magnification), click this button:

`Zoom In`

Repeat if necessary. To zoom out, click this button:

`Zoom Out`

Repeat if necessary.

Printing

You can arrange and print multiple images on a single piece of paper.

Pull down the File menu and click Print Multiple Images. In the special screen:

do the following:

- **drag images from the bar on the left onto the correct page location**
- **(optionally) click an image and apply any relevant menu commands, or;**
- **to print the images, pull down the File menu and click Print**

Re. step 3 – see your printer's manual for how to do this.

When you've previewed your image and it's ready to print, do the following:

Printing your work

Pull down the File menu and carry out the following steps:

Click here

2 Click here; select a printer

3 Optional – click here to adjust your printer's settings

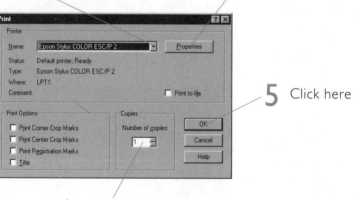

5 Click here

4 Type in the no. of copies you require

Paint Shop Pro starts printing the active image.

Index